BUSINESS ISSUES, COMPETITION AND ENTREPRENEURSHIP

SHIFT WORK

IMPACTS, DISORDERS AND STUDIES

BUSINESS ISSUES, COMPETITION AND ENTREPRENEURSHIP

Additional books in this series can be found on Nova's website under the Series tab.

Additional e-books in this series can be found on Nova's website under the eBooks tab.

BUSINESS ISSUES, COMPETITION AND ENTREPRENEURSHIP

SHIFT WORK

IMPACTS, DISORDERS AND STUDIES

WAN HE
AND
LILI YU
EDITORS

nova
science publishers
New York

Copyright © 2017 by Nova Science Publishers, Inc.

All rights reserved. No part of this book may be reproduced, stored in a retrieval system or transmitted in any form or by any means: electronic, electrostatic, magnetic, tape, mechanical photocopying, recording or otherwise without the written permission of the Publisher.

We have partnered with Copyright Clearance Center to make it easy for you to obtain permissions to reuse content from this publication. Simply navigate to this publication's page on Nova's website and locate the "Get Permission" button below the title description. This button is linked directly to the title's permission page on copyright.com. Alternatively, you can visit copyright.com and search by title, ISBN, or ISSN.

For further questions about using the service on copyright.com, please contact:
Copyright Clearance Center
Phone: +1-(978) 750-8400   Fax: +1-(978) 750-4470   E-mail: info@copyright.com.

NOTICE TO THE READER

The Publisher has taken reasonable care in the preparation of this book, but makes no expressed or implied warranty of any kind and assumes no responsibility for any errors or omissions. No liability is assumed for incidental or consequential damages in connection with or arising out of information contained in this book. The Publisher shall not be liable for any special, consequential, or exemplary damages resulting, in whole or in part, from the readers' use of, or reliance upon, this material. Any parts of this book based on government reports are so indicated and copyright is claimed for those parts to the extent applicable to compilations of such works.

Independent verification should be sought for any data, advice or recommendations contained in this book. In addition, no responsibility is assumed by the publisher for any injury and/or damage to persons or property arising from any methods, products, instructions, ideas or otherwise contained in this publication.

This publication is designed to provide accurate and authoritative information with regard to the subject matter covered herein. It is sold with the clear understanding that the Publisher is not engaged in rendering legal or any other professional services. If legal or any other expert assistance is required, the services of a competent person should be sought. FROM A DECLARATION OF PARTICIPANTS JOINTLY ADOPTED BY A COMMITTEE OF THE AMERICAN BAR ASSOCIATION AND A COMMITTEE OF PUBLISHERS.

Additional color graphics may be available in the e-book version of this book.

Library of Congress Cataloging-in-Publication Data

ISBN: 978-1-53612-460-6

Published by Nova Science Publishers, Inc. † New York

CONTENTS

Preface		**vii**
Chapter 1	The Consequences of Shift Work in Family and Social Life *Isabel S. Silva and Daniela Costa*	1
Chapter 2	Links between Shift Work, Cardiovascular Risk and Disorders *Ioana Mozos*	23
Chapter 3	Adaptation to Shift Work: The Role of an Organizational Context *Isabel S. Silva and Joana Prata*	45
Bibliography		**69**
Related Nova Publications		**89**
Index		**97**

PREFACE

Shift work has been associated to several negative consequences for the workers. In general, it can be said that the effects on health, to some extent derived from the desynchronization between working hours and the circadian system, have been the most studied by the scientific community. Chapter One aims at presenting the main impacts of shift work at the family level and social life, particularly in terms of work-family conflict, marital relationships, parenting and participation in social/community life. Chapter Two reviews the main cardiovascular disorders and risk factors associated with shift work, the main mechanisms linking shift work and cardiovascular diseases, especially hypertension, cardiac arrhythmia, coronary heart disease, stroke, arterial stiffness and early arterial aging, providing a brief description of the latest studies in the area, their implications for cardiovascular prevention, clinical practice and therapy. Chapter Three intends to present and reflect on the key strategies that can be implemented in an organizational context in order to promote adaptation to shift work.

Chapter 1 – Shift work has been associated to several negative consequences for the workers. In general, it can be said that the effects on health, to some extent derived from the desynchronization between working hours and the circadian system, have been the most studied by the scientific community. On the one hand, this time arrangement, especially if it involves night hours, working on weekends and/or rotation between shifts, can have a significant negative impact on the workers' family and social life due to the conflict between working hours and the temporal organization of family members, close friends and/or the community in general. However, under certain personal circumstances, working in a schedule different from the conventional working hours (i.e., Monday to Friday during the day) can represent advantages in this area (e.g., increased free time during the day, which can allow spending more time with small children). Compared to the effects on health, the research on the impacts of shift work with special emphasis on the social aspects has been, however, more limited.

Based on literature, this chapter aims at presenting the main impacts of shift work at the family level and social life, particularly in terms of work-family conflict, marital relationships, parenting and participation in social/community life. In addition to the literature on the topic, empirical data from three studies carried out in Portugal, wherein the association between the lack of reconciliation of working hours/shifts with the personal and social life was evaluated, will also be presented. The chapter ends with reference to the intervention possibilities, where the role, which the organizations can play in reducing work-family conflict for these workers, is also reflected. In fact, the available evidence has indicated that workers who have non-standard working hours, including shifts, when compared with workers subjected to conventional work schedules, tend to report higher work-family conflict.

Chapter 2 – Considering that cardiovascular disorders are the leading mortality causes worldwide, and the first clinical sign may be the last one, prophylactic measures deserve special attention. Industrialization and technological advancements explains the need of working during "non-standard" hours, in order to cover emergencies or the cost of some services. It was the aim of the present paper to review the main cardiovascular disorders and risk factors associated with shift work, the main mechanisms linking shift work and cardiovascular diseases, especially hypertension, cardiac arrhythmia, coronary heart disease, stroke, arterial stiffness and early arterial aging, providing a brief description of the latest studies in the area, their implications for cardiovascular prevention, clinical practice and therapy. Shift work disturbs biological rhythms, impairs nocturnal melatonin secretion, cortisol rhythmicity, leptin secretion, deregulating the immune system and enabling subclinical inflammation, insulin resistance, induces behavioral, physiological and psychosocial stress, endothelial dysfunction, lifestyle changes and dyslipidemia, possible links to cardiovascular diseases. Despite conflicting results of the studies assessing the relationship between shift work and cardiovascular risk and disorders, respectively, cardiovascular diseases should be screened and cardiovascular health should be monitored in shift workers. Measures to minimize the negative impact of disrupted circadian rhythms deserve special attention.

Chapter 3 – Shift work, especially when performed during the night, has been associated with several negative consequences from the point of view of occupational health and safety (e.g., sleep and digestive problems, fatigue, work accidents). This work schedule can also have negative impacts on social life and workers' families, especially when working time collides with socially valued periods (e.g., Sunday, end of the day).

In order to minimize such consequences, several intervention strategies have been proposed, some focused on the worker himself, others on the organization. This chapter intends to present and reflect on the key strategies that can be implemented in an organizational context in order to promote adaptation to shift work. Specifically, it aims to promote the following strategies: design of shift systems, training and information provided by the organization to employees, possibility of holding naps at work, physical resources (e.g., canteen, transport), and working time management practices in terms of human resources (e.g., degree of involvement given to workers regarding the management of their working time). Regarding this last strategy (management practices of working time), the results of empirical studies carried out in Portugal, especially in the industrial sector, will also be presented, where the relationship between the adoption of such practices and some of the effects typically associated with shift work, namely the ones regarding health and social effects, were analyzed. Anchored in this presentation, the conceptualization and operationalization of such organizational intervention strategy will also be discussed.

In: Shift Work
Editors: Wan He and Lili Yu

ISBN: 978-1-53612-460-6
© 2017 Nova Science Publishers, Inc.

Chapter 1

THE CONSEQUENCES OF SHIFT WORK IN FAMILY AND SOCIAL LIFE

*Isabel S. Silva** *and Daniela Costa*
School of Psychology, University of Minho, Braga, Portugal

ABSTRACT

Shift work has been associated to several negative consequences for the workers. In general, it can be said that the effects on health, to some extent derived from the desynchronization between working hours and the circadian system, have been the most studied by the scientific community. On the one hand, this time arrangement, especially if it involves night hours, working on weekends and/or rotation between shifts, can have a significant negative impact on the workers' family and social life due to the conflict between working hours and the temporal organization of family members, close friends and/or the community in general. However, under certain personal circumstances, working in a schedule different from the conventional working hours (i.e., Monday to Friday during the day) can represent advantages in this area (e.g., increased free time during the day, which can allow spending more time with small children). Compared to the effects on health, the research on the impacts of shift work with special emphasis on the social aspects has been, however, more limited.

Based on literature, this chapter aims at presenting the main impacts of shift work at the family level and social life, particularly in terms of

---

* Corresponding Author Email: isilva@psi.uminho.pt.

work-family conflict, marital relationships, parenting and participation in social/community life. In addition to the literature on the topic, empirical data from three studies carried out in Portugal, wherein the association between the lack of reconciliation of working hours/shifts with the personal and social life was evaluated, will also be presented. The chapter ends with reference to the intervention possibilities, where the role, which the organizations can play in reducing work-family conflict for these workers, is also reflected. In fact, the available evidence has indicated that workers who have non-standard working hours, including shifts, when compared with workers subjected to conventional work schedules, tend to report higher work-family conflict.

Keywords: shift work, work schedules, family life, social life, work-family conflict

INTRODUCTION

The working hours play a key role in the temporal organization of societies, because they structure the time available for the remaining spheres of individual's life, such as family, social or leisure spheres (Fagan, 2001). This interdependence is visible by the coordination that exists between most services, such as education and public services, with other economic activities. Indeed, both services are governed by the "conventional" work schedules, in other words, Monday through Friday, typically from 9:00 am to 5:00 pm. On the other hand, leisure activities are articulated bearing in mind the work schedules of the majority population, occurring particularly at the end of the day or on weekends. In other words, they happen especially in the "outside of work" hours for the majority of the population.

This chapter proposes to present, based on the literature review, the major impacts of shift work at the level of family and social life, particularly in terms of marital relations, parental relations and participation in social/community life. In addition, a reflection on possibilities of intervention in this area is proposed, in particular on the role that organizations can play in the reduction of work-family conflict for the shift workers, which focus on the adoption of the flexible management practices of the working time.

NON-STANDARD WORK SCHEDULES

There have been significant changes in the working world with the evolution of societies, including greater diversification of working hours. Factors such as globalization of the economy, competition among markets or the involvement of women in the labor market have triggered a diversification in terms of organizing working hours (Eurofound, 2012; Presser, 1999). In this context, organizations have felt the need to increase their operating time, with such increases extending up to 24 hours a day, 365 days per year, and involving the development of non-standard working hours (Costa, 2003; Li et al. 2014). The designation of non-standard or non-conventional work schedules has been used to characterize the hours that somehow differ from conventional or standard working hours, in other words, from Monday to Friday during business time, commonly referred to the time of "9 to 5." So, work schedules such as night shift or shift work (Boisard, Cartron, Gollac, &Valeyre, 2003; Costa, 2003) have been included in such designation.

The term "shift work" has been associated to the organization of work schedules that allow the succession of different people or teams, and can extend up to 24 hours daily (Costa, 1997). Many shift systems are characterized by several aspects (see, for example, Costa, 1997 or Thierry & Jansen, 1998). For example, shift systems may or may not integrate switching teams for different shifts. When workers are allocated to the same shift every day (e.g., work in the evening from 2:00 pm to 10:00 pm), they are assigned fixed shifts, and when workers have to periodically switch between different shifts (e.g., switch between morning, evening and night shift each week), they are assigned rotating systems. Rotating systems may also differ in terms of speed and direction of rotation. The start and end of shifts or a combination of the number of working days and days off in the week are other aspects that characterize the shifts systems.

Non-standard work schedules have increased over the last years in the European Union as shown by the evolution from 2010 to 2015. According to the fifth European Working Conditions Survey, in 2010, 51% of the active population in EU worked at least one Saturday per month, 26% at least one Sunday per month, 19% worked during the night, and 17% worked in the shifts (Eurofound, 2012). Five years later, in 2015, the sixth European Working Conditions Survey indicated that 52 percent worked at least one Saturday per month, 30% at least one Sunday per month, 19% worked during the night, and 21% worked in the shifts (Eurofound, 2015). Considering the context of the United States in 2010, the percentage of workers in shifts was 28.7% (Alterman, Luckhaupt, Dahlhamer, Ward, & Calvert, 2013).

Although the shift work is a solution that allows the extension of the working time of the organizations, the literature (e.g., Costa, 2003; Silva, 2012; Smith, Folkard, & Fuller, 2003) has highlighted several negative effects of shift work for workers, especially when the work schedule conflicts with the biological rhythms and/or with the family and social activities. On the other hand, shift work may also represent some advantages for workers, which will be discussed in the next section of this chapter.

SHIFT WORK

Different work schedules may represent advantages and disadvantages for workers. Although the literature tends to emphasize the "dark side" of the shift work, this time arrangement represents advantages for organizations and can, under certain circumstances, also represent advantages for workers and their families. Indeed, this work schedule can represent financial advantages (where the shift allowance stands out) or the level of reorganization/temporal flexibility (Silva, Prata, Ferreira, & Veloso, 2014; West, Mapedzahama, Ahern, & Rudge, 2012). This temporal reorganization could offer more free time during the day, which can be advantageous in terms of access to services or the social relations level and/or family. For example, the study of Agosti, Andersson, Ejlertsson, and Janlöv (2015), in which thirteen nurses were interviewed, noted that shift work could be viewed as a positive thing owing to the combination of different options that it allowed. For example, it lets spend more time with the kids, and offers more equality in the home and childcare. Other studies have also indicated a greater involvement by fathers in activities at home when there was a difference in the work schedules of the couple. For example, Barnett and Gareis (2007) studied 55 families with children, and found that when mothers worked at night, instead of during daytime, fathers were more involved in the childcare and exhibited greater coexistence and more involvement in the life and activities of children. The study of Presser (1994) also identified different involvement levels in domestic activities in function of the work schedules and gender. For example, it was observed that the number of hours, for which the husbands were involved with tasks, traditionally regarded as "feminine," increased significantly only when they worked in non-daytime fixed or rotating schedules and the respective women worked during daytime.

Carneiro and Silva (2015) gathered, from a group of 110 health professionals (mostly women), several advantages related to shift work. The flexibility of timetables, the non-existence of routines, the free time during the week and the weekend, the days off during the week, and the work-family balance were the main advantages for these professionals related to the shift work.

However, the literature has revealed that when shift work systems imply night work, either fixed or in rotation shifts and/or in periods valued socially, difficulties may occur at the level of health, social and/or family life besides organizational level (Costa, 1997; Silva, 2012; Smith et al. 2003). Carneiro and Silva (2015) also gathered, from the participants, some disadvantages of shift work besides the advantages presented previously, where the interference with sleep and with family and friends stands out, as well as the physical and psychological wear.

In terms of the advantages and disadvantages associated to the shift work, it should be noted that different schedules/shifts tend to be associated with to different aspects. For example, while the night shifts are often associated to sleep complaints and financial advantages (shift bonus), at the same time, the evening shift tends to be associated to greater interference with family time and less interference with the rest/sleep (Silva et al. 2014). The study of Silva et al. (2014), which sought to identify the advantages and disadvantages of shift work from the perspective of the workers themselves (textile workers), indicated that the negative aspects (e.g., negative impacts on the health and well-being) were more prevalent in shifts involving night work, on the contrary from the positive aspects (e.g., work/life interface). Specifically, the proportion of positive and negative aspects in each shift was as follows: morning (60.3% versus 39.7%), evening (59.9% versus 45.1%), night shift (41.8% versus 58.2%) and a rotating system involving nights (24.3% versus 75.7%). As we shall see in the following point, rotating shifts, particularly if they involve night work, weekend work and/or irregularity, also present more difficulties from the family and social point of view.

Despite the growing interest in researching shift work and its impacts, the study of the health consequences has been privileged in detriment of the consequences on social and family life (Ljoså & Lau, 2009; Matheson, O'Brien, & Reid, 2014; Perrucci et al. 2007). For example, in the recent review of the literature of Matheson et al. (2014), in which 118 studies published between 1980 and 2013 were analyzed, the authors concluded that the research on shift work was focused mainly on the impacts of shift work on sleep and health of workers, not focusing deeply, therefore, on the impacts in other spheres of life of individuals.

FAMILY LIFE AND SOCIAL LIFE

Generally speaking, complaints associated to the shift work of family/social perspective derive from the desynchronization of working hours with the other members of the family and of society, and it may generate additional difficulties in marital, parental and terms in the living/social participation (Dhande & Sharma, 2011; Handy, 2010; Li et al. 2014; Rosenbaum & Mazlan, 2009; Silva, 2012; Silva, Prata, & Ferreira, 2014; Šimunić & Gregov, 2012). As pointed out by Costa (2003), people involved in night shifts and/or rotation shifts suffer high pressure from society and their families, as temporal organization is a constant problem that carries negative impacts on marital relations, parental roles and the education of children.

The study of Demerouti, Geurts, and Bakker (2004) examined the relationship between two aspects of working hours, in particular, the pattern (fixed or shift work) and chronological position in the week in relation to the work-family conflict, burnout levels, the attitudes of work, organizational commitment and absenteeism. More than 3000 Dutch military personnel participated in the study. The results indicated that the rotation of working hours was associated to unfavorable work attitudes, i.e., less job satisfaction, greater intent to turnover and lower performance. On the other hand, it was observed that the working hours of the most valued periods from the family and social point of view (e.g., weekend) were associated to greater work-family conflict.

Wight, Raley, and Bianchi (2008) found evidence that parents, who worked at non-standard times (evening: from 4:00 pm to midnight; night: from midnight to 8:00 am), had less availability to carry out activities together with their children, spent less time with the spouse, they slept less and watched less television. However, the authors found that parents, who were working in non-standard shifts, spent more time alone with their children than parents who worked in standard hours of work. Ljoså and Lau (2009) examined the impacts of different shifts in social and family life based on a sample of approximately 1700 employees of a Norwegian oil and gas company. The authors found some reports of problems caused by shift work on family and social life in most participants, varying by different systems of shifts, and the most harmful of them were the shifts that encompassed a day and a night at sea and those that included rotation.

Camerino et al. (2010), noting that the literature examining directly the effects of working hours in work-family conflict was scarce, studied the impacts of different work schedules on work-family relationship, the possible association between a preventive culture and a smaller work-family conflict and the association between specific indicators and the work-family conflict. The authors found evidence that different work schedules have different impacts on the work-family relationship, and that the schedules that involve night and irregular schedules are the more damaging ones. Also, the work-family conflict was associated to burnout, sleep and absenteeism. The authors also concluded that the development of a preventive culture in the workers, who work in night shifts and irregular shifts, is effective in reducing the work-family conflict, increased well-being and performance.

Other authors have compared the work family conflict between shift workers and diurnal workers such as Tuttle and Garr (2012) or Mauno, Ruokolainen, and Kinnunen (2015). In both cases, it was observed that shift workers, compared to diurnal workers, had greater work-family conflict. In the study of Strzemecka et al. (2013), 700 shift workers were interviewed. Almost half of the participants (43%) reported that the shift work influenced their family life. The authors concluded that the shift work negatively influenced the family life of workers, regardless of marital status, age and whether or not they had children.

Kunst et al. (2014) proposed to investigate to what extent different timetables of shift work could explain the variance in positive and negative repercussions on work-family and family-work relationships compared to "conventional" work schedules. About 2000 Norwegian nurses participated in the study, divided into four working hours: normal working hours and three shift work schedules (day and night shift, night shift only or rotating three shifts – morning, evening and night). Diurnal workers reported less work-family conflict than employees who work on shift schedules. In turn, the rotating system with night was the one that exhibited greater work-family conflict of the four working hours.

In short, the evidence presented earlier points to the fact that shift work is associated to a greater work-family conflict in comparison to the day job, although there may be substantial differences between the various shift systems. Notwithstanding the previous conclusion, as mentioned above regarding the benefits, shift work can contribute, however, to a greater involvement of the father/husband at home, including in childcare when both members of the couple work.

Marital Relations

As for the impacts on married life are concerned, White and Keith (1990) found a higher probability of divorce in the shift workers, major problems in sexual relations and in relations with the children, as well as lower levels of marital bliss. Smith and Folkard (1993) studied the perceptions of the spouses of approximately 50 shift workers (all men) regarding the impacts that the work schedule had on their lives. The results indicated that most of the spouses were unhappy with the shift schedule of their husbands. The study of Mott, Mann, McLoughlin, and Warwick (1965), based on more than 1000 shifts workers, also all male, reinforceed the previous results. This study, based on the approach of the roles, examined the extent to which a particular shift schedule facilitated or interfered with the performance of various roles in the family context as compared to daytime schedules, considering the perspective of both members of the couple. Considering the role of the husband, aspects such as the ability to provide company and protection to the spouse, support in domestic life, moments of conviviality and joint decision making or sex were accounted. With the exception of domestic life, which, generally, benefited from shift work hours as compared to daytime schedules, the remaining aspects have been considered worse. On the other hand, considering the perspective of more than 650 wives interviewed, the results indicated that shift work, when compared to the daytime schedules, made aspects like sexual relations, the ability to provide emotional support and companionship to the spouse or making certain household chores more difficult.

Other more recent studies have also sought to evaluate the impact of the work schedules on the marital life point of view. For example, the study of Perry-Jenkins, Goldberg, Pierce, and Sayer (2007) was based on a sample of 132 couples together for at least a year and expecting their first child. It is worth noting that all the participants worked before the birth of their child, and intended to return to work until after 6 months from the birth. The objective of this study was to investigate how nonstandard working hours, especially afternoon and night shifts or a rotating system, were associated to depressive symptoms in the couple and relationship conflicts. It was observed that afternoon and night shifts were associated to higher levels of depressive symptoms in the 6 months after the birth of the child, in both the mother and the father. The levels of conflict in the relationship, in the 6 months after giving birth, were determinants of depressive symptoms in both the mother and the father, i.e., with higher levels of conflicts, more depression symptoms arose.

Similarly, Maume, and Sebastian (2012) found evidences that men, who worked in shifts, reported that their work schedules affected the quality of their relationships, while their wives commented that the work-family conflict affected the marital relationship. In other words, for men, the working hours were responsible for the quality of their marital relationship, while for the women, greater work-family conflicts reduced the quality of this relationship.

Minnotte, Minnotte, and Bonstrom (2015), using data from the 2002 National Study of the Changing Workforce, which contained data from 1,046 married men and 776 married women, found a negative association between work-family conflicts and marital satisfaction, finding that greater work-family conflict levels resulted into lower levels of marital satisfaction.

More recently, Gracia and Kalmijn (2016) conducted a study with data collected in the 2003 Spanish Time Use Survey to analyze how the work schedules were associated to the family, marital and parental relations and family leisure activities. The authors came to the conclusion that night shifts were negatively associated to family time and couple time, but the same wasn't true regarding the time parents spent with their children.

In short, the previous study suggested that certain atypical working hours can put increased demands on the management of the couple's life.

Parental Relationships

Regarding the impacts of work schedules in parental relationships, Volger, Ernst, Nachreiner, and Hänecke (1988) examined the amount and the chronological position of the common free time among parents of different schedule systems and their children of different ages. 700 policemen working in different shifts systems as well as their children, in pre-school or school age, with their common time budget (the free time in common among both), participated in study. The results indicated that pre-school children had more free time with their parents, whereas for children in school age, the common free time was considerably reduced.

Additionally, Barton, Aldridge, and Smith (1998) compared the emotional state of children with parents working in daytime schedules and parents working in shift schedules. They concluded that shift schedules can be stressful for the family and affect the emotional state of the children. In a study by Strazdins, Clements, Korda, Broom, and D'Souza (2006), the association between the nonstandard work schedules and family relationships along with their well-being was evaluated. To this end, they compared families where parents worked on conventional schedules with the families where the parents worked in nonstandard shifts. It is worth noting that children belonging to these families were between 2 and 11 years old. Parents, who were working in nonstandard times, reported worse family structure, more depression symptoms and less effective parenting. It was observed that the children of these workers had more social and emotional difficulties as compared to the children of day workers. Davis, Crouter, and McHale (2006) studied the impacts of the shift work schedules on parental relationships in accordance with the reports of parents and teens. The results showed that children of mothers, who worked in shifts, reported greater intimacy with them as compared to the children of mothers, who worked in daytime schedules. In the case of fathers working in shifts, their children reported just the opposite, i.e., less intimate relationship between them. In this case, the parents also reported less knowledge of the daily activities of their children. The authors also found evidence that when both parents were working in shifts and had a high conflict relationship, intimate relationships with their children were harmed.

In a study by Daniel, Grzywacz, Leeker, Tucker, and Han (2009), the interrelationships of nonstandard mothers (evening, night and variable) and the presence of existing behavior problems in early childhood and over time were examined. It has been observed that this kind of work arrangement on the part of the mothers was a predictor of behavior problems in the children at the age of 24 and 36 months. A study by Han and Miller (2009) examined the relationship between parental work schedules and problems in teenage kids, especially depression. The results indicated that mothers, who worked night hours, had lower home environment quality and took less meals together, which was significantly associated to an increased risk of depression in teenage kids. In this context, using the same database, Han, Miller, and Waldfogel (2010) assessed risky behaviors in adolescents, and found that those whose mothers worked night shifts more often had riskier behaviors than teens whose mothers worked normal working hours. In the same vein, Rosenbaum and Mazlan (2009) found negative association between shift schedules and parent-child interaction, marital quality, frequency of family dinners and parental health, including paternal depression. The results also showed that the shift schedules had greater effects on the behavior of children when mothers, rather than fathers, work in unconventional shifts. More recently, in the meta-analysis conducted by Li et al. (2014), significant associations were observed between nonstandard working hours and adversities in childhood development. These adversities were measured through depression symptoms of the parents, parental interaction, low quality and proximity between parents and children, and less favorable home environment.

Other studies have evaluated the impacts of the work schedules of parents and the weight of the children. In a study by Miller and Han (2008), the relationship between the nonstandard working hours of the mother and the overweight of teenage children was evaluated. It was observed that the body mass index (BMI) of adolescents and the risk of overweight increased significantly when mothers worked in nonstandard shifts. Despite the results, the income of families constituted a critical aspect in this association with reduced incomes related to a greater risk of overweight among adolescents. A study by Morrissey, Dunifan, and Kalil (2011), in turn, have not confirmed the association between the nonstandard working shifts (night, weekend or variable) of the mother and the BMI of children, but noticed an association between the children BMI and the number of hours worked by the mother, i.e., more hours of work increase the risk of an increased BMI in children.

In this follow-up, Champion et al. (2012) evaluated the effects of nonstandard working hours (shift schedules and working after 6:00 pm, including work at home, overnight or on weekends) by the mother, the father or both could have on overweight and obesity of children of 9 years of age based on a longitudinal study of 557 women and children. It was observed that the overweight and obesity in children were associated to the completion of work in nonstandard hours by the father but not the mother. When both parents were working in nonstandard hours, a greater tendency of overweight and obesity in children was observed.

In another strand, Han and Fox (2011) focused on the relationship between the work schedules of parents and the relations with their children, the home environment and activities after school and how those relationships could be related to "child cognitive outcomes." The study was based on a sample of 7105 children, who were followed for 13 to 14 years since birth. The results showed that when mothers worked for several years in a night shift, the children had lower reading performance, whereas when the parents worked for several years on a night shift, the children had lower grades in mathematics. The results also indicated that when mothers worked in the afternoon or the evening, the children had a slower trajectory in mathematics. As for rotating shifts, when practiced by the mothers, the children had significantly higher notes in reading, while in the case of fathers, the children had higher grades in math. The measurement tests conducted helped to understand the effects that the afternoon and evening shifts by mothers had on their children's cognitive outcomes through three factors: mother knowledge, meals together, and performing household chores after school for the kids. Regarding the maternal knowledge about the child, a positive association in reading and math results was observed, along with the possibility to decrease the negative association between afternoon and evening shifts by the mother and low academic results. Similarly, it was observed that fewer meals held together in a family can explain the relationship between maternal duty and low academic results. Finally, performing household chores for the kids after school could help explain the slower trajectory in math when mothers worked afternoon or evening shifts.

In short, the observation of the previous literature suggests that one of the critical aspects in understanding the influence of parents' work schedules and their children is related to the common free time these schedules allow and the quality of that time.

Social Life

The hours of the day and the weekdays are not the same from a social point of view. Indeed, the structure of the "social time" in industrialized countries is largely synchronized with the work schedules of the majority of the population. Thus, the relative periods in the evening and on the weekends (especially Sunday) are the most valued from a social life/community and family point of view, as also indicated by several empirical studies (e.g., Baker, Ferguson, & Dawson, 2003; Craig & Brown, 2014; Hornberger & Knauth, 1993; Martin, Wittmer, & Lelchook, 2011; Staines & Pleck, 1984). The differentiation of financial compensation depending on the different periods worked (e.g., night, Sunday, holidays) reflects the value of such differential recovery time (Walker, 1985).

A study by Baker et al. (2003) illustrated comprehensively, as far as we are concerned, the differential value of time in different spheres of life. In total, 220 workers participated in the study, distributed equitably in two groups – daytime schedule workers and shift workers – paired by age, gender, marital status and parental status. Participants were asked to point out the degree of preference to perform a given activity in each hour of the week, bearing in mind the following dimensions: social, work, leisure and family. Both groups of workers, in shift and daytime schedules, expressed a similar preference for performing activities within the social, leisure and family spheres. Specifically, in both groups, the favorite periods correspond to the end of the day during the working days of the week and on weekends. Regarding the preference for "working time," although both groups had expressed a preference for the same period – in this case, working days of the week, during the day – yet it was observed that shift workers have a greater flexibility in the use of time in this sphere.

In the light of the results obtained considering the appreciation of the time, it is understandable that the shift systems involving work on weekends, in the evening, at night and/or an irregularity regarding work hours (given the greater difficulty in planning activities) are the ones that can present more difficulties in terms of social and family gathering. Indeed, even though shift workers may have more free time during the day, yet this will tend not to match the other family members, friends and community, which may lead to a "social desynchronization" between the occupation time of these workers and the social environment.

We conclude this topic with the presentation of results obtained in three studies conducted in Portugal, which also help to illustrate the differences between different work schedules regarding family and social impact (Table 1). In this Table, the mean values on the scale developed by Silva (2008) are presented to assess the lack of conciliation between work schedules and the personal as well as social activities outside of the organizational context. This scale is made up of six items (e.g., *"your work schedule leaves you enough time to be with family and close friends?"*), these being answered on a Likert scale of 5 points (1) "totally disagree" to (5) "totally agree" (the alpha Cronbach's value stood at .91). The higher the score on the scale, the greater the ability of the participants in reconciling the activities outside their organizational context with the work schedule. As can be seen in the Table, the higher values are associated to the morning shift, which allows free time at the end of day/night, whereas the lowest are associated to shifts that require work during this period, limiting therefore the availability to activities outside the organization.

Table 1. Comparison of the perceptions of conciliation regarding working time and life outside of the organizational context due to shifts in three studies carried out in Portugal

Studies	Sample (sector)	Comments	Morning shift M (SD)	Evening shift M (SD)	Night shift M (SD)	Rotating shift M (SD)	F	Comparisons post hoc[+]
Prata & Silva (2013)	490 workers (Industry)	3 fixed shifts: Morning – 6:00 am to 2:30 pm Evening – 2:30 pm to 11:00 pm Night – 11:00 pm to 6:00 am	3,47 (0,81)	2,88 (0,77)	3,88 (0,77)	2,95 (0,75)	41.037***	Morning ≠ Evening
Carneiro & Silva (2015)	110 health professionals (Health)	All participants were subject to rotating shifts, but were divided as to more often than was allocated a particular shift	3,03 (0,79)	2,81 (0,65)	2,88 (0,94)	------	0,76	There are no ≠
Silva & Keating (2016)	373 workers (Industry)	3 fixed shifts: Morning - 6:00 am to 2:00 pm Evening – 2:00 pm to 10:00 pm Night - 10:00 pm to 6:00 am	4,12 (0,69)	3,79 (0,75)	3,79 (0,90)	------	6.524**	Morning ≠ Evening and Night

* $p < .05$; ** $p < .01$; *** $p < .001$.
[+]This column lists the shifts that differed in significant statically manner.

CONTRIBUTIONS TO THE INTERVENTION AND CONCLUSION

Despite shift work schedules making possible the organizations' growth, this model isn't free of difficulties, including from the family and social point of views, as mentioned throughout this chapter. Therefore, it is important to identify and reflect the possibilities of intervention that might promote the adaptation to this work arrangement. This chapter ends with a reference to some of these possibilities and a reflection on the importance of flexibility in this area.

Härmä and Ilmarinen (1999) presented some "practical countermeasures" to promote the health and well-being of older shift workers. These countermeasures were divided into two groups: design of shift work systems and occupational health care. In the first group, the authors gathered strategies like the *increase in the flexibility given to the workers*, the increase in time offs and breaks, the decrease in the amount of night work and shifting workers who have been performing night works for several years to daytime hours. In the second group, they included measures such as increased medical surveillance, advice on coping strategies and *individual solutions*.

Demerouti et al. (2004), in turn, suggested that the shift hours that correspond to periods with great value at a family and social level should be avoided in order to minimize the work-family conflict. On the other hand, the shifts involving rotation should be designed with a *high degree of individualization and flexibility*.

Later, Root, and Wooten (2008), in order to contribute to the human resources management literature that discusses the work-family conflict, proposed some recommendations to manage this conflict regarding parents and shift workers. Among the various given recommendations are the following: human resources managers should be a part of the working groups that work in nonstandard times to help with the implementation of family friendly policies, redefine *flexible working arrangements* for shift workers, support the extension of childcare beyond conventional period, create a group of shift working parents to support each other and ultimately build an organizational culture that values *flexibility a*nd high quality relationships.

Pagnan, Lero, and MacDermid Wadsworth (2011) also presented some recommendations to reduce the work-family conflict that exists in shift work. Some of these suggestions go through allowing parents to have access to a mobile phone in order to maintain contact with their children, especially during night shifts, extend mid shift pauses to enable the parents to go home at mealtime or the time to put the kids to sleep and make a recreation area to receive the family during breaks from work.

Dhande and Sharma (2011) also proposed a number of recommendations to reduce the impact of shift work, which include the reduction of night work and shift work, *greater flexibility in work schedules*, the possibility of night workers to have a hot meal, prolonging the opening of cafeteria for 24 hours, providing training to employees about ways that could reduce the negative effects of shift work and quick shift changes should be avoided. In the same vein, Estryn-Béhar and Van der Heijden (2012) conducted a study with approximately 26000 nurses in Europe, and they stressed the importance of some intervention strategies to decrease the effects of shift work: increasing the operating time of the institutions/services providing care for children, *participation of workers on the elaboration of shift schedules*, nap breaks during night shifts, reduction of changing shifts at short notice and organization of working hours with attention to social support and team spirit.

Simunić and Gregov (2012) also proposed some ways to minimize the negative impacts of shift work, from which we underline the knowledge of working hours in advance and a certain *degree of flexibility to accommodate the needs of workers*.

As previously described, there are several possibilities for action proposed in the literature to promote an adaptation to shift work in general and the reduction of work-family conflict in particular. In this context, we underline the flexibility and the employee involvement in managing the temporal aspects of work, referred to by a number of authors (we marked such recommendations in italics throughout this section). Indeed, if we consider that many difficulties that can arise in family and/or social sphere will depend on the personal circumstances of each employee (e.g., presence of children, age of children, employment status of spouse, spousal work hours, social support from family and/or community), the possibility that the employee could somehow control his/her working hours (e.g., choose the shift, switch between shifts) would facilitate the management of work/life interface. Such "flexibility and involvement culture" can be developed by organizations that adopt shift work within its policies and management practices of the temporal aspects of work (for example, an organization can allow/encourage some level of employee involvement in choosing the schedule at the time of admission, while other organizations may not permit).

REFERENCES

Agosti, M. T., Andersson, I., Ejlertsson, G., & Janlöv, A. C. (2015). Shift work to balance everyday life – a salutogenic nursing perspective in home help service in Sweden. *BMC Nursing, 14*(2), 1-11.

Alterman, T., Luckhaupt, S. E., Dahlhamer, J. M., Ward, B. W., & Calvert, G. M. (2013). Prevalence rates of work organization characteristics among workers in the U.S.: Data from the 2010 National Health Interview Survey. *American Journal of Industrial Medicine, 56*(6), 647–659.

Baker, A., Ferguson, S., & Dawson, D. (2003). The perceived value of time: Controls versus shiftworkers. *Time & Society, 12*(1), 27-39.

Barnett, R. C., & Gareis, K. C. (2007). Shift work, parenting behaviors, and children's socioemotional well-being: A within-family study. *Journal of Family Issues, 28*(6), 727 – 748.

Barton, J., Aldridge, J., & Smith, P. (1998). The emotional impact of shift work on the children of shift workers. *Scandinavian Journal of Work and Environmental Health, 24*(Suppl. 3), 146-150.

Boisard, P., Cartron, D., Gollac, M., & Valeyre, A. (2003). *Time and work: Duration of work*. Ireland: European Foundation for the Improvement of Living and Working Conditions.

Camerino, D., Sandri, M., Sartori, S., Conway, P. M., Campanini, P., & Costa, G. (2010). Shiftwork, work-family conflict among Italian nurses, and prevention efficacy. *Chronobiology International, 27*(5) 1105−1123.

Carneiro, L., & Silva, I. S. (2015). Trabalho por turnos e suporte do contexto organizacional: Um estudo num centro hospitalar [Shift work and organizational support: A study in a hospital]. *International Journal on Working Conditions, 9*, 142-160.

Champion, S. L., Rumbold, A R., Steele E. J., Giles, L. C., Davies, M. J., & Moore V. M. (2012). Parental work schedules and child overweight and obesity. *International Journal of Obesity, 36*, 573-580.

Craig, L., & Brown, J. (2014). Weekend and leisure time with family and friends: Who misses out?, *Journal of Marriage and Family,76*(4), 710-727.

Costa, G. (1997). The problem: Shitwork. *Chronobiology International, 14*(2), 89-98.

Costa, G. (2003). Shift work and occupational medicine: an overview. *Occupational Medicine, 53*, 83-88.

Daniel, S. S., Grzywacz, J. G., Leerkes, E., Tucker, J., & Han, W. J. (2009). Nonstandard maternal work schedules during infancy: Implications for children's early behavior problems. *Infant Behavior and Development, 32*(2), 195-207.

Davis, K. D., Crouter, A. C., & McHale, S. M. (2006). Implications of shift work for parente-adolescent relationships in dual-earner families. *Family Relations, 55,* 450-460.

Demerouti, E., Geurts, S. A., & Bakker, A. B. (2004). The impact of shiftwork on workhome conflict, job attitudes and health. *Ergonomics, 47*(9), 987-1002.

Dhande, K. K., & Sharma, S. (2011). Influence of shift work in process industry on workers' occupational health, productivity, and family and social life: An ergonomic approach. *Human Factors and Ergonomics in Manufactoring & Service Industries, 21*(3), 260-268.

Estryn-Behar, M., Van der Heijden, B., & the NEXT Study Group. (2012). Effects of extended work shifts on employee fatigue, health, satisfaction, work/family balance, and patient safety. *Work, 41*, 4283-4290.

European Foundation for the Improvement of Living and Working Conditions – Eurofound. (2012). *Fifth European Working Conditions Survey.* Luxembourg: Publications office of the European Union.

European Foundation for the Improvement of Living and Working Conditions – Eurofound. (2015). *First findings: Sixth European Working Conditions Survey.* Publications office of the European Union.

Fagan, C. (2001). Time, money and the gender order: Work orientations and working time preferences in Britain. *Gender, Work and Organization, 8*(3), 239-266.

Gracia, P., & Kalmijn, M. (2016). Parents' family time and work schedules: The split-shift schedule in Spain. *Journal of Marriage and Family, 78*(2), 401-415.

Han, W. J., & Fox, L. E. (2011). Parental work schedules and children's cognitive trajectories. *Journal of Marriage and Family, 73*, 962-980.

Han, W. J., & Miller, D. P. (2009). Parental work schedules and adolescent depression. *Health Sociology Review, 18*(1), 36–49.

Han, W. J., Miller, D. P., & Waldfogel, J. (2010). Parental work schedules and adolescent risky behaviors. *Developmental Psychology, 46*(5), 1245–1267.

Handy, J. (2010). Maintaining family life under shiftwork schedules: A case study of a New Zealand petrochemical plant. *New Zealand Journal of Psychology, 39*(1), 29-37.

Härmä, M., & Ilmarinen, J. E. (1999). Towards the 24-hour society – new approaches for aging shift workers? *Scandinavian Journal of Work and Environmental Health, 25*(6), 610-615.

Hornberger, S., & Knauth, P. (1993). Interindividual differences in the subjective valuation of leisure time utility. *Ergonomics, 36*(1-3), 255-264.

Kunst, J. R., Løset, G. K., Hosøy, D., Bjorvatn, B., Moen, B. E., Magerøy, N., et al. (2014). The relationship between shift work schedules and spillover in a sample of nurses. *International Journal of Occupational Safety and Ergonomics, 20*(1), 139-147.

Li, J., Johnson, S. E., Han, W., Andrews, S., Kendall, G., Stradzins, L., et al. (2014). Parents' nonstandard work schedules and child well-being: A critical review of the literature. *Journal of Primary Prevention, 35,* 53-73.

Ljosâ, C. H., & Lau, B. (2009). Shiftwork in the Norwegian petroleum industry: Overcoming difficulties with family and social life a cross sectional study. *Journal of Occupational Medicine and Toxicology, 4*(22).

Matheson, A., O'Brien, L., & Reid, J. A. (2014). The impact of shiftwork on health: A literature review. *Journal of Clinical Nursing, 23,* 3309–3320.

Martin, J. E., Wittmer, J. L. S., & Lelchook, A. M. (2011). Attitudes towards days worked where Sundays are scheduled. *Human Relations, 64,* 901-926.

Maume, D. J., & Sebastian, R. A. (2012). Gender, nonstandard work schedules, and marital quality. *Journal of Family and Economic Issues, 33,* 477-490.

Mauno, S., Ruokolainen, M., & Kinnunen, U. (2015). Work–family conflict and enrichment from the perspective of psychosocial resources: Comparing Finnish healthcare workers by working schedules. *Applied Ergonomics, 48,* 86-94.

Miller, D. P., & Han, W.-J. (2008). Maternal nonstandard work schedule and adolescent overweight. *American Journal of Public Health, 98,* 1495-1502.

Minnotte, K. L., Minnotte, M. C., & Bonstrom, J. (2015). Work– family conflicts and marital satisfaction among US workers: Does stress amplification matter? *Journal of Family and Economic Issues, 36*(1), 21–33.

Morrissey, T. W., Dunifon, R. E., & Kalil, A (2011). Maternal employment, work schedules, and children's body mass index. *Child Development, 82,* 66-81.

Mott, P. M., Mann, F. C., McLoughlin, Q., & Warwick, D. P. (1965). *Shift work: The social, psychological and physical consequences.* Ann Arbor, Michigan: The University of Michigan Press.

Pagnan, C. E., Lero, D. S., & MacDermid Wadsworth, S. M. (2011). It doesn't always add up: examining dual-earner couples' decision to off-shift. *Community, Work & Family, 14*(3), 297-316.

Perry-Jenkins, M., Goldberg, A, Pierce, C. P., & Sayer, A J. (2007). Shift work, role overload, and the transition to parenthood. *Journal of Marriage and Family, 69*, 123-138.

Perrucci, R., MacDermid, S., King, E., Tang, C., Brimeyer, T., Ramadoss, K., et al. (2007). The significance of shift work: Current status and future directions. *Journal of Family and Economic Issues, 28*, 600-617.

Prata, J., & Silva, I. S. (2013). Efeitos do trabalho em turnos na saúde e em dimensões do contexto social e organizacional: Um estudo na indústria electrónica [Shiftwork Effects on Health and on Social and Organizational Life: A Study in the Electronics Industry]. *Revista Psicologia: Organizações e Trabalho, 13*(2), 141-154.

Presser, H. B. (1994). Employment schedules among dual-earner spouses and the division of household labor by gender. *American Sociological Review, 59*, 348-364.

Presser, H. B. (1999). Toward a 24-hour economy. *Science, 11*(284), 1778-1779.

Root, L. S., & Wooten, L. P. (2008). Time out for family: Shift work, fahers, and sports. *Human Resource Management, 47*(3), 481-499.

Rosenbaum, E., & Morett, C. R. (2009). The effect of parents' joint work schedules on infants' behavior over the first two years of life: Evidence from the ECLSB. *Maternal and Child Health Journal, 13*(6), 732-744.

Silva, I. S. (2008). *Adaptação ao trabalho por turnos* [Adaptation to shift work]. Dissertação de Doutoramento em Psicologia do Trabalho e das Organizações [PhD in Work and Organizational Psychology]. Braga: Universidade do Minho.

Silva, I. S. (2012). *As condições de trabalho no trabalho por turnos. Conceitos, efeitos e intervenções [The working conditions in shift work. Concepts, effects and interventions]*. Lisboa: Climepsi Editores.

Silva, I. S., Prata, J., & Ferreira, A. I. (2014). Horários de trabalho por turnos: Da avaliação dos efeitos às possibilidades de intervenção [Shiftwork schedules: From effect's evaluation to intervention possibilities]. *International Journal on Working Conditions, 7*, 68-83.

Silva, I. S., Prata, J., Ferreira, A. I., & Veloso, A. (2014). Shiftwork experience: Worker's vision of its impacts. In P. Arezes et al. (Eds.), *Occupational Safety and Hygiene II* (pp. 651-656). London: Taylor & Francis Group.

Silva, I. S., & Keating, J. (2016). Shift Work: Impact on sleep, family and social life, and satisfaction with work schedule. In P. Arezes et al. (Eds.), *Occupational Safety and Hygiene IV* (pp. 265-268). London: Taylor & Francis Group.

Šimunić, A., & Gregov, L. (2012). Conflict between work and family roles and satisfaction among nurses in different shift systems in Croatia: A questionnaire survey. *Arhiv Za Higijenu Rada i Toksikologiju, 63*(2), 189-197.

Smith, L., & Folkard, S. (1993). The perceptions and feelings of shiftworkers partners. *Ergonomics, 36*(1-3), 299-305.

Smith, C. S., Folkard, S., & Fuller, J. A. (2003). Shiftwork and working hours. In J. C. Quick & L. E. Tetrick (Eds.), *Handbook of occupational health psychology* (pp. 163-183) (2nd ed.). Washington, DC: American Psychological Association.

Staines, G. L., & Pleck, J. H. (1984). Nonstandard work schedules and family life. Journal of *Applied Psychology, 69*(3), 515-523.

Strazdins, L., Clements, M. S., Korda, R. J., Broom, D. H., & D'Souza, R. M. (2006). Unsociable work? Nonstandard work schedules, family relationships, and children's well-being. *Journal of Marriage and Family, 68*, 394 – 410.

Strzemecka, J., Pencula, M., Owoc, A., Szot, W., Strzemecka, E., Jablonski, M., et al. (2013). The factor harmful to the quality of human life – shift-work. *Annals of Agricultural and Environmental Medicine, 20*(2), 298-300.

Tuttle, R., & Garr, M. (2012). Shift work and work to family fit: Does schedule control matter? *Journal of Family Economic Issues, 33*, 261-271.

Thierry, H., & Jansen, B. (1998). Work time and behaviour at work. In P. J. D. Drenth, H. Thierry & C. J. de Wolff (Eds.), *Handbook of work and organizational psychology* (Vol. 2: Work Psychology) (2nd ed., pp. 89-119). East Sussex: Psychology Press.

Volger, A., Ernst, G., Nachreiner, F., & Hänecke, K. (1988). Common free time of family members under different shift systems. *Applied Ergonomics, 19*(3), 213-218.

Walker, J. (1985). Social problems of shiftwork. In S. Folkard & T. Monk (Eds.), *Hours of work: Temporal factors in work-scheduling* (pp. 211-225). Chichester: John Wiley & Sons Ltd.

West, S., Mapedzahama, V., Ahern, M., & Rudge, T. (2012). Rethinking shiftwork: mid-life nurses making it work. *Nursing Inquiry, 19*(2), 177-187.

White, L., & Keith, B. (1990). The effect of shift work on the quality and stability of marital relations. *Journal of Marriage and the Family, 52,* 453-462.

Wight, V. R., Raley, S. B., & Bianchi, S. M. (2008). Time for children, one's spouse and oneself among parents who work nonstandard hours. *Social Forces, 87*(1), 243–271.

In: Shift Work
Editors: Wan He and Lili Yu

ISBN: 978-1-53612-460-6
© 2017 Nova Science Publishers, Inc.

Chapter 2

LINKS BETWEEN SHIFT WORK, CARDIOVASCULAR RISK AND DISORDERS

Ioana Mozos[*]
Department of Functional Sciences, Discipline of Pathophysiology
"Victor Babes" University of Medicine and Pharmacy,
Timisoara, Romania

ABSTRACT

Considering that cardiovascular disorders are the leading mortality causes worldwide, and the first clinical sign may be the last one, prophylactic measures deserve special attention. Industrialization and technological advancements explains the need of working during "non-standard" hours, in order to cover emergencies or the cost of some services. It was the aim of the present paper to review the main cardiovascular disorders and risk factors associated with shift work, the main mechanisms linking shift work and cardiovascular diseases, especially hypertension, cardiac arrhythmia, coronary heart disease, stroke, arterial stiffness and early arterial aging, providing a brief description of the latest studies in the area, their implications for cardiovascular prevention, clinical practice and therapy. Shift work disturbs biological rhythms, impairs nocturnal melatonin secretion, cortisol rhythmicity, leptin secretion, deregulating the immune system

---

[*] Correspondence to: Ioana Mozos, MD, PhD, "Victor Babes" University of Medicine and Pharmacy, Department of Functional Sciences, Discipline of Pathophysiology, Timisoara, Romania. E-mail: ioanamozos@yahoo.de.

and enabling subclinical inflammation, insulin resistance, induces behavioral, physiological and psychosocial stress, endothelial dysfunction, lifestyle changes and dyslipidemia, possible links to cardiovascular diseases. Despite conflicting results of the studies assessing the relationship between shift work and cardiovascular risk and disorders, respectively, cardiovascular diseases should be screened and cardiovascular health should be monitored in shift workers. Measures to minimize the negative impact of disrupted circadian rhythms deserve special attention.

INTRODUCTION

Cardiovascular disorders are the leading mortality causes worldwide. The first clinical sign may be the last one and this is the reason why prophylactic measures deserve special attention.

Industrialization and technological advancements have created the need of working outside the standard hours (from 9 to 5), some institutions operating 24 hours each day, in order to cover emergencies or the cost of some services, to meet the needs of flexibility of the workforce, to enable commercial competitiveness and to increase and optimize productivity (Di Lorenzo et al., 2003; Asare-Anane et al., 2015). Shift work has become one of the most common work schedules (Asare-Anane et al., 2015) and more than 15% of the European and American workers are exposed to this complex lifestyle (Son et al., 2015). Shift work can be defined as employment in any work schedule that is not a regular daytime schedule (Li et al., 2016). Most of the shift workers are involved in protective services, health, sales, street cleaning, waste collection and services or primary industry. Healthcare services during night time is provided in Europe by medical personnel working on night-call duty, following a regular daytime shift, which is a stressful situation (Rauchenzauner et al., 2009). Shift work is mandated by employer, is better payed, enables better child or family care arrangements or time for school. The benefits of shift work are associated with health and safety risks to the employees, considering that worktime patterns are becoming more diversified, flexible, irregular and unhealthy (Asare-Anane et al., 2015). Shift work disturbs biological and physiological rhythms, suppresses nocturnal melatonin, impairs cortisol rhythmicity, leptin secretion, deregulating the immune system, induces behavioral, physiological and psychosocial stress, possible links to cardiovascular diseases (Puttonen et al., 2010; Mozos, Filimon, 2013; Son et al., 2015; Gasier et al., 2016). Cardiac autonomic function, influenced by the sleep-wake cycle, with a relative dominance of the sympathetic system during daytime and of the parasympathetic system during night-time, is impaired due to shift work, with a higher sympathetic activity during sleep and a lower parasympathetic activity during shift work, increasing the risk of cardiovascular disease (Rauchenzauner et al., 2009). Psychological disturbances after night work were associated with impaired cardiovascular and endocrine responses in healthy nurses (Munakata et al., 2001). There are wide variations in psychological adaptation to night shift work and the factors predicting effective adaptations are poorly understood (Steptoe, 2009). Metabolic and nutritional disturbances related to shift work enable several comorbidities, such as central obesity, hypertension, dyslipidemia, endothelial dysfunction, which are risk factors for cardiovascular disease. High job strain enables progression of atherosclerosis, demonstrated by subclinical markers of atherosclerosis in the aorta, cerebral and carotid artery in Japanese factory workers (Michikawa et al., 2008). Previous studies have demonstrated accelerated atherosclerosis, elevated inflammatory markers related to the atherosclerotic process, and endothelial dysfunction in shift workers (Costa, 2010; Puttonen et al., 2009; Suessenbacher et al., 2011).

The relationship between shift work and cardiovascular morbidity has been studied for a long time and by several authors, but the results are conflicting.

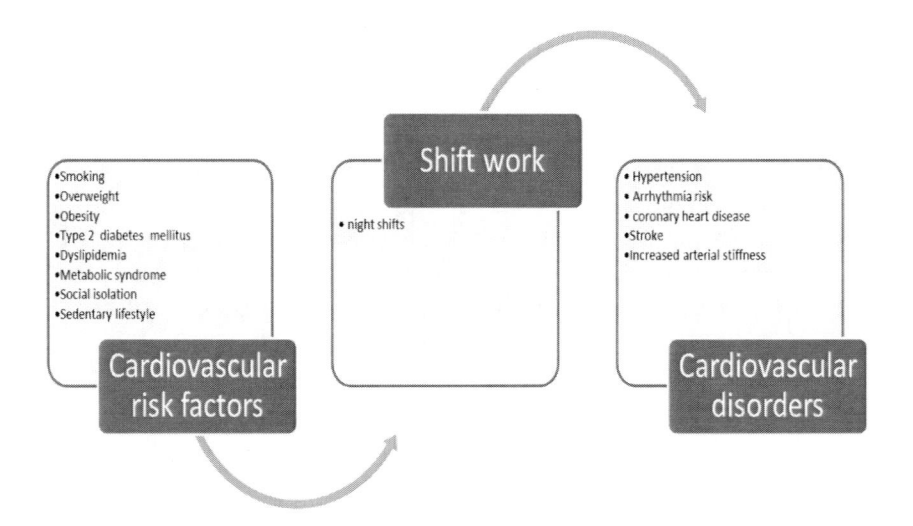

Figure 1. Cardiovascular risk factors and disorders related to shift work.

AIM

Considering the worldwide high cardiovascular morbidity and mortality, it was the aim of the present paper to review the main cardiovascular disorders and risk factors associated with shift work, the main mechanisms linking shift work and cardiovascular diseases, providing a brief description of the latest studies in the area, their implications for cardiovascular prevention, clinical practice and therapy.

SHIFT WORK AND CARDIOVASCULAR RISK FACTORS

Shift and night workers have a higher prevalence of cardiovascular risk factors, such as overweight and obesity, hypertension, smoking, sedentary lifestyle and social isolation (Figure 1).

Smoking: Work environment may influence smoking behavior according to several studies carried out in the United States and Europe. Independent of educational level, shift workers are more prone to start smoking and the risk to stop smoking is lower in shift workers, especially in those working long hours (Van Amelsvoort et al., 2006; Jang et al., 2013) and the prevalence of smoking increases with the number of hours worked (Radi et al., 2007). Night workers smoked more than day workers (Biggi et al., 2008), with a tendency to smoke in the workplace (Van Amelsvoort et al., 2006). Individuals who work long hours or whose jobs involve a high level of manual labor have difficulties in trying to quit smoking (Kassel et al., 2003; Cho et al., 2013). Considering that physically demanding jobs are usually carried out by men, women in such positions use smoking in order to be accepted into a male-dominated work (Radi et al., 2007). The higher smoking prevalence in long work hours employees was explained by low socioeconomic position and marital status in a study including 2,044 male subjects who responded to a questionnaire of the Korean Labor and Income Panel Study (Jang et al., 2013). Low job satisfaction and precarious employment are also related to smoking and nicotine dependence (Peretti-Watel et al., 2009; Chon et al., 2010). A recent prosective study showed that future shift workers smoked more than future day workers before they began to work at night (Nabe-Nielsen et al., 2008).

Tobacco smoking accelerates atherogenesis, by enhancing oxidative modifications of LDL, decreasing HDL levels and causing endothelial dysfunction, is prothrombotic by increasing platelet adhesiveness, and causes hypoxia. Considering that women metabolize nicotine faster than men, the risk is higher in women.

Smoking is a cardiovascular risk factor that can be controlled. Healthy lifestyle choices include smoking avoidance (Yu et al., 2016). Smoking may affect also nonsmokers because passive smoking and second-hand smoke are also associated with an increased cardiovascular risk. Intervention programs to decrease smoking prevalence must consider employment type, job satisfaction and work-related factors (Jang et al., 2013).

Overweight and obesity: The prevalence of obesity increased worldwide, related to changes in traditional lifestyle factors, diet and physical activity and is associated with increased cardiovascular mortality and morbidity and a substantial economic burden (Knutson et al., 2007). Body mass index (BMI) was significantly higher in shift workers compared to non-shift workers according to a study including 113 rotating shift workers and 87 non-shift workers, and predicted waist to hip ratio (WHR), high sensitive C reactive protein and coronary risk (Asare-Anane et al., 2015). Night workers had significantly higher BMI than day workers, and intra-individual comparison among the workers who were day workers at the beginning of their employment and became later night workers, showed a significant increase in BMI (Biggi et al., 2008). Shift working for more than 5 years significantly increased BMI (van Amelsvoort et al., 1999). Shift work was directly responsible for increased body fatness in a study including 319 glucose tolerant male individuals working in the chemical industry and was indirectly associated with higher blood pressure levels and some features of metabolic syndrome (Di Lorenzo et al., 2003). Several other previous studies demonstrated correlations between BMI and shift work (Karlsson et al., 2001; Ye et al., 2013; Silva-Costa et al., 2016; Yoon et al., 2016), but other studies found no relationship between shift work and obesity or BMI (Nakamura et al., 1997; Ghiaswand et al., 2006). BMI, the most common and simple method to measure obesity, has several limitations, especially for individuals with intermediate values, considering accuracy in assessing the degree of adiposity (Son et al., 2015). Gasier et al. investigated 53 young, male submariners before and after a 3-month routine submarine patrol, exposed to rotating shift work, reduced sleep, confined space, void of sunlight and limited exercise equipment, and found no significant weight changes or worsening of the cardiometabolic health (Gasier et al., 2016). Shift workers had also higher waist-to-hip ratio (WHR) than day workers, as a sign of abdominal fat accumulation, independently of body mass index (Di Lorenzo et al., 2003). Weight gain occurs especially in late-shift workers (evening and night), cleanroom and offshore workers under continued exposure to day-night shift work (Parkes et al., 2002). Peplonska et al. conducted a cross-sectional study among 724 female nurses and midwives and reported significant associations between cumulative night shift work and body mass index, waist and hip circumference, waist to hip ratio, demonstrating that both current and cumulative night work was associated with obesity in women performing eight or more night shifts/month (Peplonska et al., 2015). Son et al assessed the total body fat percentage using dual-energy X-ray absorptiometry in 2,952 Korean male manual workers, and found a statistically significant increase in obesity risk in shift workers (Son et al., 2015).

An unhealthy lifestyle, including irregular eating patterns, especially during night shifts and low-quality diet, enable weight gain (Asare-Anane et al., 2015; Nea et al., 2015). Several studies did not demonstrate a significant association between sedentary work and obesity (Shrestha et al., 2016). Melatonin suppression during shift work induces insulin resistance, glucose intolerance and sleep disturbance, leading to obesity (Cipolla-Neto et al., 2014). Circadian rhythm disruption impairs the metabolic responses to feeding, due to insulin resistance, alters leptin secretion favoring food intake, dysregulating immunity and enabling systemic inflammation (Castanon-Cervantes et al., 2010; Gasier et al., 2016). Loss of cortisol rhythmicity results in hyperactivity of the hypothalamic-pituitary-adrenal axis, leading to long term elevated cortisol levels, causing obesity (Manenschijn et al., 2011). The increased leptin/adiponectin ratio in obsese patients and shift workers causes a proinflammatory state, considering that leptin is pro-inflammatory, upregulating tumor necrosis factor alpha and interleukin-6, and adiponectin is anti-inflammatory, downregulating the expression and release of proinflammatory immune mediators (Lopez-Jaramillo et al., 2014; Gasier et al., 2016). The proinflammatory state is associated with insulin resistance and endothelial dysfunction (Lopez-Jaramillo et al., 2014; Gasier et al., 2016). The interactions between angiotensin II and leptin/adiponectin imbalance may mediate development of type 2 diabetes mellitus and cardiovascular disorders in obese patients (Lopez-Jaramillo et al., 2014). Forced physical exercise produces negative physiological adaptations to stress, releasing corticotropin-releasing hormone (Yanagita et al., 2007). Long work time (over 60 hours per week in Korean male workers) increases also the risk of obesity (Magee et al., 2011). Food, not just the light-dark cycle, is able to drive the human internal clock, especially the circadian clock in the liver (Ribas-Latre et al., 2016). Several tissues function under circadian control, including the heart, skeletal muscle and white adipose tissue (Ribas-Latre et al., 2016). The circadian system is sensitive to changes in food composition: high fat diets are able to lenghten the circadian period, advancing the phase of the liver clock by 5 hours (Ribas-Latre et al., 2016). On the other hand, the decrease in average sleep duration occured in the same time period as the increase in the prevalence of obesity and diabetes (Knutson et al., 2007). On the other hand, chronic work stress may suppress appetite and increase physical activity, leading to weight loss (Bara et al., 2009).

Overweight and obesity were associated with absenteeism, disability pension and overall work impairment (Shrestha et al., 2016). A workplace-based weight loss program: the workplace POWER program, improved work-related outcome in 110 overweight and obese male shift workers (Morgan et al., 2012). Educational measures, informing shift workers about healthy lifestyle choices and lowering cardiovascular risk by a healthy diet, low in saturated and trans fat, refined carbohydrates and sugar-sweetened beverages, with a focus on wholegrain products, unsaturated fats, vegetables, fruit and fish, and vigorous aerobic physical activity of at least 15 minutes for 5 days/week, according to the 2016 European Guidelines on cardiovascular disease prevention in clinical practice (Piepoli et al., 2016) and several other studies (Yu et al., 2016), could be very helpful in shift workers. The cardiovascular risk factors were independent of type of shift or practice of physical activity in a study including 57 male truck drivers, of whom 31 worked irregular shifts (Marqueze et al., 2013).

Type 2 Diabetes mellitus: Diabetes is highly prevalent at working ages, especially in truck drivers (Riva et al., 2016). Night work was found as a potential risk factor for type 2 diabetes mellitus in a longitudinal study including 15,105 Brazilian civil servants, and was also associated with an increased body mass index, waist circumference, and, in women, with increased fasting plasma glucose, glycated hemoglobin and 2-hour plasma glucose (Silva-Costa et al., 2016). Impaired glucose metabolism in shift workers is related to the reduced sleep period, common in shift workers (Knutson et al., 2007; Asare-Anane et al., 2015). Hyperglycemia enables synthesis of advanced glycosilated endproducts, which induce secretion of inflammatory cytokines and occurence of chronic complications. Suwazono et al. found a significantly higher risk of developing diabetes for workers on alternating shift work than for regular day work (Suwazono et al., 2006).

Dyslipidemia: Total cholesterol, triglycerides, low density and very low density lipoproteins were significantly higher among shift and night workers compared to controls, related to reduced sleep and disruption of biological rhythms or eating during the night shift (Di Lorenzo et al., 2003; Biggi et al.,

2008; Asare-Anane et al., 2015). Significant elevations in the serum levels of cholesterol, glucose, uric acid and potassium have been reported during the first week after a night shift, not related to changes in dietary habits or other lifestyle factors (Theorell et al., 1976).

Metabolic syndrome: The cluster of independent risk factors termed metabolic syndrome, including central obesity, hypertension, dyslipidemia and impaired glucose metabolism, is more prevalent in shift and night workers compared to day workers (Biggi et al., 2008). Prospective studies have demonstrated an increased incidence of the metabolic syndrome in shift workers (Kawachi et al., 1995), related, probably, to insulin resistance, melatonin suppression and elevated cortisol levels. Jermendy et al. reported higher systolic blood pressure, body mass index and lower HDL level in shift workers compared to daytime workers, associated with a less healthy lifestyle (Jermendy et al., 2012).

Social isolation: Stress affects social lives and individuals may retract from social interactions, may become hostile and irritable (Sandi et al., 2015). Social isolation, stress at work and in family life, hostility, depression, anxiety contribute to the development of cardiovascular disorders, with a worse prognosis, acting as a barrier to treatment adherence (Piepoli et al., 2016). There is evidence in the scientific literature of the adverse psychological effects of shift work, including social isolation (Admi et al., 2008).

Inflammation and Shift Work

Inflammation may be the link between shift work and several disorders, including obesity, diabetes, atherosclerosis, coronary heart disease, stroke, gastric ulcer and cancer (Castanon-Cervantes et al., 2010). Subclinical inflammation plays a critical role in all stages of atherosclerosis, starting with the nascent lesion to the atheromatous plaque (Libby et al., 2002). Inflammatory markers include cytokines and chemokines, soluble adhesion molecules and acute phase reactants (Davis et al., 2012). Alterations of the sleep-wake cycle impairs the number of the circulating lymphocytes, natural killer cells and antibody titers, and increases inflammatory cytokines such as interleukin-6, C reactive protein and TNF-alpha (Castanon – Cervantes et al., 2010).

High sensitive C reactive protein, an independent risk markers for cardiovascular diseases, increases plasminogen activator inhibitor-1 expression and activity, indicating lower plasminolysis, enabling atherosclerosis, and promoting complement activation causing constriction of the coronary vessels (Langrand et al., 1999; Davis et al., 2012).

Sleep Duration in Shift Workers and Cardiovascular Disorders

Both long and short sleep durations are associated with atherosclerosis and cardiovascular disorders (Wolff et al., 2008; Yoshioka et al., 2011). Yoshioka et al. demonstrated an association between long sleep duration (at least 9 hours of daily sleep) and arterial stiffness in a study including 4,268 Japanese employees (Yoshioka et al., 2011). Compared to a reference of 8 hour sleep, both shorter (5 hours) and longer ($\geq$ 10 hours) sleep durations were associated with a higher intima-media thickness in a German study including 2,437 participants (Wolff et al., 2008). Participants of the later study indicated their daily sleep duration as sum of night and afternoon sleep (Wolff et al., 2008). Night shifts cause sleep deprivation, mental stress and impair coronary microcirculation (Kubo et al., 2011).

The mechanisms explaining the relationship between sleep duration and cardiovascular disorders are not fully understood. Short sleep duration causes adverse endocrinologic, immunologic and metabolic effects (Akerstedt et al., 2003; Knutson et al., 2007). Laboratory and epidemiological studies suggest that sleep loss may be associated with the increased prevalence of diabetes and obesity, involving, al least, 3 pathways: impaired glucose metabolism, upregulation of appetite and decreased energy expediture (Knutson et al., 2007).

SHIFT WORK AND CARDIOVASCULAR DISORDERS

Shift Work and Hypertension

The association between shift work and hypertension is controversial (Rauchenzauner et al., 2009; Rotenberg et al., 2016). Asare-Anane et al. found no significant differences for mean systolic and diastolic blood pressure for shift and non-shift workers, probably due to adaptation to biological rhythms, active work and consumption of cocoa products (Asare-Anane et al., 2015). Systolic blood pressure and heart rate were lower during night shift than during day shift, and folllowing a night shift than following a day shift, despite similar physical activity level in a study including 18 healthy nurses engaged in a modified rapid shift rotation system (Munakata et al., 2001).

Cross-sectional and cohort studies revealed an association between shift work and hypertension (Cassat et al., 2015). Hypertension was more prevalent among shift workers aged 30 - 49 years, probably due to job related stress and considering that more stressful jobs are given to younger employees (Asare-Anane et al., 2015). Shift workers on counter-clockwise rotation were characterized by higher systolic blood pressure, urinary catecholamines excretion and plasma levels of triglycerides and glucose compared to shift workers of clockwise rotation (Di Lorenzo et al., 2003). Napping during night work may be a protective factor for hypertension, related to melatonin secretion, blood pressure control and dipping patterns (Rotenberg et al., 2016). Several studies reported higher sleeping blood pressure in night than in day shift work (Munakata et al., 2001). Rauchenzauner et al. revealed higher sleeping blood pressure in night shift work than in day shift work, higher 24 hours diastolic blood pressure and a higher diastolic blood pressure during night time (Rauchenzauner et al., 2009). The heterogeneity of the studies, several confounding factors and the difficulties in achieving a suitable comparison groups do not allow firm clinical conclusions (Cassat et al., 2015).

Shift Work and Arrhythmia Risk

Night shift work influences blood pressure, heart rate, heart rate variability and catecholamine secretion (Rauchenzauner et al., 2009). Changes in heart rate variability, a noninvasive marker of cardiac autonomic control, and arrhythmias, such as sinus tachycardia and bradicardia, sinus pause, premature atrial and ventricular contractions, and supraventricular tachycardia, have been reported during and after night shift, related to stress and increased sympathetic tone (Adams et al., 1998; Rauchenzauner et al., 2009). Rauchenzauner et al. evaluated the effects of a 24 hours physicians on-call duty (night shift) on 24 hours electrocardiogram, heart rate variability, blood pressure and serum and urine stress markers, respectively, compared with a regular day at work, and found a higher rate of **ventricular premature beats** during early morning, a greater diastolic blood pressure throughout 24 hours as well as during sleep time and higher noradrenaline excretion during physicians on-call duties (Rauchenzauner et al., 2009). Van Amelsvoort et al investigated 49 subjects starting shift work, and noticed an increased incidence of premature ventricular contractions after 1 year of shift work, related to a change in arrhythmogeneity, but not of cardiac autonomic control (Van Amelsvoort et al., 2001). The increase in frequency of premature ventricular contractions is related to the numer of days worked on night shift (Van Amelsvoort et al., 2001). Night shifts induce short-term activations of the sympathetic system, associated with the occurence of ventricular and supraventricular tachyarrhythmias or premature beats (Rauchenzauner et al., 2009).

The **QT interval**, the electrocardiographic expression of ventricular depolarization and repolarization, is a marker of ventricular arrhythmia risk (Al-Khatib et al., 2003; Rautaharju et al., 2009). The **Tpeak-Tend interval** (TpTe), the interval from the T-wave peak to the end of the T wave, has been accepted as a measure of transmural dispersion of repolarization related to arrhythmogenesis (Gupta et al., 2008; Zhao et al., 2010). The QT interval was prolonged in 6 and 24 hours work-shift employees and also related to unpredictable and non-standard working hours (Meloni et al., 2013). Conduction and repolarization disorders were more frequently observed among 6 hours work-shift employees (Meloni et al., 2013) and the QTc interval tended to increase with age among 8 hours shift workers (Meloni et al., 2010). Mozos and Filimon performed 12-lead ECG in 60 shift workers during the morning, afternoon and night shift and found a circadian pattern of QT and Tpeak-Tend intervals: the QT and Tpeak-Tend interval (TpTe) were prolonged during the night and morning shift, with the afternoon shift as reference (Mozos, Filimon, 2013). QT and TpTe prolongation was highest in hypertensive, overweight and obese participants, smokers and those with prolonged exposure to shift work (Mozos, Filimon, 2013). Participant age, hypertension and body mass index were independent predictors of QT interval prolongation, while age and smoking status predicted TpTe prolongation (Mozos, Filimon, 2013).

Shift Work and Coronary Heart Disease

A higher incidence of coronary heart disease was recorded in night workers (Biggi et al., 2008). A systematic review by Frost et al., including 14 studies, showed limited epidemiological evidence for a causal relation between shift work and ischemic heart disease (Frost et al., 2009). Kubo et al investigated 36 women nurses who underwent transthoracic Doppler echocardiography after working a nightshift and found a lower coronary flow reserve than on a regular work day, demonstrating an impaired coronary microcirculation after nightshift work (Kubo et al., 2011). Vetter et al. conducted a prospective study including 189,158 initially healthy registered nurses, with a history of rotating night shift work, followed up for 24 years, and found an increase of coronary heart disease risk, including nonfatal myocardial infarction, angiogram-confirmed angina pectoris, coronary artery bypass graft surgery, stents and angioplasty (Vetter et al., 2016). Mixed results were found for the association between different types of shift work and acute myocardial infarction among 1,891shift workers with and without pre-existing ischemic heart disease (Wang et al., 2016). Travelling work, with at least 3 nights per week away from home, was positively associated with acute myocardial infarction among men with pre-existing ischemic heart disease (Wang et al., 2016). Hermansson et al. conducted a case-control study in two geographical areas in Sweden, including 1,542 subjects and concluded that shift work was associated with an increased risk of case fatality among male shift workers after the first myocardial infarction (Hermansson et al., 2015).

Shift Work and Stroke

Stroke is one of the leading causes of mortality, and 10% of all strokes occur in individuals 18-50 years of age, the main productivity period (Li et al., 2016). Shift work was considered a risk factor for stroke (Li et al., 2016).

Several studies showed a minor positive relationship between shift work and cerebrovascular mortality (Li et al., 2016), but Hermansson et al did not fiind a higher risk of shift workers for ischemic stroke, compared to day workers in a study including 138 shift workers and 469 day workers less than 65 years (Hermansson et al., 2007). On the other hand, Earnest et al. showed recently, that circadian rhythm disruption associated with shift irregular work schedules, interact with nonmodifiable cardiovascular risk factors to modulate stroke-induced infarct volume and sensorimotor deficits (Earnest et al., 2016).

Shift Work, Arterial Stiffness, Endothelial Dysfunction and Arterial Aging

Vascular stiffness, a dynamic property based on both vascular function and structure, can be assessed by pulse wave velocity (PWV) measurement. An association between high job strain and elevated PWV was noticed before in several studies (Michikawa et al., 2008; Belkic et al., 2004). More advanced structural vascular wall changes can be assessed by measuring intima-media thickness (Yoshioka et al., 2011).

Shift work has been demonstrated to predict early arterial aging in a study including 61 workers employed in a car harness manufacturing enterprise (Mozos, Filimon, 2013). Early arterial aging was detected in 70% of the study participants, and the number of shifts was associated with pulse wave velocity and endothelial dysfunction (Mozos, Filimon, 2013).

Shift work accelerates the atherosclerotic process and the effects of shift work on subclinical atherosclerosis are observable in men before 40 years of age, according to a study including 1,543 young adults and carotid artery intima-media thickness (Puttonen et al., 2009). In women, no association was found between shift work and markers of carotid atherosclerosis (Puttonen et al., 2009).

CONCLUSION

Night shift is also called "grave-shift" considering its effect on life expectancy, and, cardiovascular disorders could be an important link. Night and shift work are associated with cardiovascular risk and may predict cardiovascular disorders due to interference with circadian rhythms and lifestyle, over-activity of the sympathetic system, disruption of circadian blood pressure and activation of inflammatory cytokines.

Elimination of shift work is an effective measure to workers health management, or, at least, flexible work arrangements, self-scheduling and avoiding permanent night work, especially in physically and mentally demanding professions. Considering socioeconomic factors, this is, probably, not possible. Measures to minimize the negative impact of disrupted circadian rhythms deserve special atention. Workplace interventions in shift workers should consider educational programs, focusing stress management strategies, cardiovascular health, risk factors and early symptoms, healthy lifestyle, workplace-based weight loss programs in overweight and obese workers and interventions for increasing physical activity. Shift workers need medical follow-up focused on cardiovascular risk and lifestyle factors, blood pressure monitoring, electrocardiographic canges, vascular health and cardiac symptoms.

Future studies should focus on finding the type of shift work mostly impairing cardiovascular health, identification of individuals more susceptible to negative cardiovascular effects of shift work and interventions able to minimize the negative effects of shift work.

REFERENCES

[1] Adams, S. L., Roxe, D. M., Weiss, J, et al. (1998). Ambulatory blood pressure and Holter monitoring of emergency physicians before, during, and after a night shift. *Acad Emerg Med*, 5(9): 871-7.

[2] Admi, H., Tzischinsky, O., Epstein, R., et al. (2008). Shift work in nursing: is really a risk factor for nurses health and patients safety? *Nurs Econ*, 26(4): 250-7.

[3] Akerstedt, T., Nilsson, P. M. (2003). Sleep as restitution: an introduction. *J Intern Med*, 254(1): 6-12.

[4] Al-Khatib, S. M., Allen La Pointe, N. M., Kramer, J. M., et al. (2003). What clinicians should know about the QT interval. *JAMA*, 289: 2120-7.

[5] Asare-Anane, H., Abdul-Latif, A., Kwaku Ofori, E., et al. (2015). Shift work and the risk of cardiovascular disease among workers in cocoa processing company, Tema. *BMC Res Notes*, 8: 798-813.

[6] Bara, A. C., Arber, S. (2009). Working shifts and mental health – findings from the British Household Panel Survey (1955-2005). *Scand J Work Environ Health Finland*, 35(5): 361-7.

[7] Belkic, K. L., Landbergis, P. A., Schnall P. L., et al. (2004). Is job strain a major source of cardiovascular disease risk? *Scand J Work Environ Health,* 30(2): 85-128.

[8] Biggi, N., Consonni, D., Galluzo, V., et al. (2008). Metabolic syndome in permanent night workers. *Chronobiol Int*, 25(2): 443-54.

[9] Cassat, M., Wuerzner, G., Burnier, M. (2015). Shift work and night work: what effect on blood pressure? *Rev Med Suisse*, 11(485): 1648-54.

[10] Castanon – Cervantes, O., Wu, M., Ehlen, J.C., et al. (2010). Dysregulation of inflammatory responses by chronic circadian disruption. *J Immunol*, 185(10): 5796-805.

[11] Cho, Y. S., Kim, H. R., Myong, J. P., et al. (2013). Association between work conditions and smoking in South Korea. *Saf Health Work*, 4(4): 197-200.

[12] Chon, S. H., Kim, J. Y., Cho, J. J., et al. (2010). Job characteristics and occupational stress on health behavior in Korean workers. *Korean J Fam Med*, 31(6): 444-52.

[13] Cipolla-Neto, J., Amaral, F. G., Afeche, S. C., et al. (2014). Melatonin, energy metabolism, and obesity. A review. *J Pineal Res*, 56: 371-81.
[14] Costa G. (2010). Shift work and health: current problems and preventive actions. *Saf Health Work*, 1: 112-23.
[15] Davis, F. J., Vidyasagar, S., Maiya, A. G. (2012). C-reactive protein and coronary heart disease – risk marker or risk factor? *J Clin Sci Res*, 1: 178-86.
[16] Di Lorenzo, L., De Pergola, G., Zocchetti, C., et al. (2003). Effect of shift work on body mass index: results of a study performed in 319 glucose-tolerant men working in a Southern Italian industry. *Int J Obes Relat Metab Disord*, 27(11): 1353-8.
[17] Earnest, D. J., Neuendorff, N., Coffman, J., et al. (2016). Sex differences in the impact of shift work schedules on pathological outcomes in an animal model of ischemic stroke. *Endocrinology*, 157(7): 2836-43.
[18] Frost, P., Kolstad, H. A., Bonde, J. P. (2009). Shift work and the risk of ischemic heart disease – a systematic review of the epidemiologic evidence. *Scand J Work Environ Health*, 35(3): 163-79.
[19] Gasier, H. G., Young, C. R., Gaffney-Stomberg, E., et al. (2016). Cardiometabolic health in submariners returing from a 3-month patrol. *Nutrients*, 8(2): pii: E85.
[20] Ghiaswand, M., Heshmat, R., Golpira, R., et al. (2006). Shift work and risk of lipid disorders: a cross-sectional study. *Lipids Health Dis*, 5: 9.
[21] Gupta, P., Patel, C., Patel, H., et al. (2008). Tp-e/QT ratio as an index of arrhythmogenesis. *J Electrocardiol*, 41: 567-74.
[22] Hermansson, J., Gillander Gadin, K., Karlsson, B., et al. (2007). Ischemic stroke and shift work. *Scand J Work Environ Health*, 33(6): 435-39.
[23] Jang, S. M., Ha, E. H., Park, H., et al. (2013). Relationship between work hours and smoking behaviors in Korean male wage workers. *Ann Occup Med*, 25(1): 35- 43.
[24] Jermendy, G., Nadas, J., Hegyi, I., et al. (2012). Assessment of cardiometabolic risk among shift workers in Hungary. *Health Qual Life Outcome*, 10: 18.
[25] Hermansson, J., Gillander Gadin, K., Karlsson, B., et al. (2015). Case fatality of myocardial infarction among shift workers. *Int Arch Occup Environ Health*, 88(5): 599-605.
[26] Karlsson, B., Knutsson, A., Lindahl, B. (2001). Is there an association between shift work and having a metabolic syndrome? Results from a

population-based study of 27,485 people. *Occup Environ Med*, 58: 747-52.

[27] Kassel, J. D., Stroud, L. R., Paronis, C. A. (2003). Smoking, stress, and negative affect: correlation, causation, and context across stages of smoking. *Psychol Bull*, 129: 270-304.

[28] Kawachi, I., Colditz, G. A., Stampfer, M.J., et al. (1995). Prospective study of shift work and risk of coronary heart disease in women. *Circulation*, 92: 3178-82.

[29] Knutson, K. L., Spiegel K., Penev P., et al. (2007). The metabolic consequences of sleep deprivation. *Sleep Med Rev*, 11: 163-78.

[30] Kubo T., Fukuda S., Hirata K., et al. (2011). Comparison of coronary microcirculation in female nurses after day-time versus night-time shifts. *Am J Cardiol*, 108(11): 1665-8.

[31] Langrand, W. K., Visser, C. A., Hermens, W. T., et al. (1999). C-reactive protein as a cardiovascular risk factor: more than an epiphenomenon? *Circulation*, 100(1): 96-102.

[32] Li, M., Huang, J. T., Tan, Y., et al. (2016). Shift work and risk of stroke: A meta-analysis. *Int J Cardiol*, 214: 370-3.

[33] Libby, P., Ridker, P. M., Maseri, A. (2002). Inflammation and atherosclerosis. *Circulation*, 105: 1135-43.

[34] Lopez-Jaramillo, P., Gomez-Arbelaez, D., Lopez-Lopez, J., et al. (2014). The role of leptin/adiponectin ratio in metabolic syndrome and diabetes. *Horm Mol Biol Clin Investig*, 18(1): 37-45.

[35] Magee, C. A., Caputi, P., Iverson, D. C., et al. (2011). Short sleep mediates the association between long work hours and increased body mass index. *J Behav Med*, 34(2): 83-91.

[36] Manenschijn, L., Van Kruysbergen, R. G. P. M., De Jong, F. H., et al. (2011). Shift work at young age is associated with elevated long-term cortisol level and body mass index. *J Clin Endocrinol Metab*, 96(11): E1862-5.

[37] Marqueze, E. C., Ulhoa, M. A., Moreno, C. R. (2013). Effects of irregular-shift work and physical activity on cardiovascular risk factors in truck drivers. *Rev Saude Publica*, 47(3): 497-505.

[38] Meloni, M., Setzu, D., Del Rio, A., et al. (2013). QTc interval and electrocardiographic changes by type of shift work. *Am J Ind Med*, 56(10): 1174-9.

[39] Meloni, M., Del Rio, A., Setzu, D., et al. (2010). Electrocardiogram changes in shift workers. *Med Lav*, 101(4): 286-92.

[40] Michikawa, T., Nishiwaki, Y., Nomiyama, T., et al. (2008). Job strain and arteriosclerosis in three different types of arteries among male Japanese factory workers. *Scand J Work Environ Health*, 34(1): 48-54.
[41] Morgan, P. J., Collins, C. E., Plotnikoff, R. C., et al. (2012). The impact of a workplace-based weight loss program on work-related outcomes in overweight male shift workers. *J Occup Environ Med*, 54(2): 122-7.
[42] Mozos, I., Filimon, L. (2013). QT and Tpeak-Tend interval in shift workers. *J Electrocardiol*, 46: 60-65.
[43] Mozos, I., Filimon, L. (2013). Arterial age and shift work. *Int J Collab Res Int Med Pub Health*, 5(5): 340-7.
[44] Munukata, M., Ichi, S., Nunokawa, T., et al. (2001). Influence of night shift on psychologic state and cardiovascular and neuroendocrine responses in healthy nurses. *Hypertens Res*, 24(1): 25-31.
[45] Nabe-Nielsen, K., Garde, A. H., Tuchsen, F., et al. (2008). Cardiovascular risk factors and primary selection into shift work. *Scand J Work Environ Health*, 34: 206-12.
[46] Nakamura, K., Shimai, S., Kikuchi, S., et al. (1997). Shift work and risk factors for coronary heart disease in Japanese blue - collar workers: serum lipids and antropometric characteristics. *Occup Med (Lond)*, 47(3): 142-6.
[47] Nea, F. M., Kearney, J., Livingstone, M. B., et al. (2015). Dietary and lifestyle habits and the associated health risks in shift workers. *Nutr Res Rev*, 28(2): 143-66.
[48] Parkes, K. R. (2002). Shift work and age as interactive predictors of body mass index among offshore workers. *Scand J Work Environ Health*, 28: 64-71.
[49] Peplonska, B., Bukowska, A., Sobala, W. (2015). Association of rotating night shift work with BMI and abdominal obesity among nurses and midwives. *PloS One*, 10(7): e0133761.
[50] Peretti-Watel, P., Constance, J., Seror, V., et al. (2009). Working conditions, job dissatisfaction and smoking behaviours among French clerks and manual workers. *J Occup Environ Med*, 51(3): 343-50.
[51] Piepoli, M. F., Hoes, A. W., Agewall, S., et al. (2016). 2016 European Guidelines on cardiovascular disease prevention in clinical practice. *Eur J Prev Cardiol*, 23(11): NP1-NP96.
[52] Puttonen, S., Harma, M., Hublin, C. (2010). Shift work and cardiovascular disease – pathways from circadian stress to morbidity. *Scand J Work Environ Health*, 36: 96-108.

[53] Puttonen, S., Kivimäki, M., Elovainio, M., et al. (2009). Shift work in young adults and carotid artery intima-media thickness: The Cardiovascular Risk in Young Finns study. *Atherosclerosis*, 205(2): 608-13.

[54] Rauchenzauner, M., Ernst, F., Hintringer, F., et al. (2009). Arrhythmias and increased neuro-endocrine stress response during physicians night shifts: a randomized cross-over trial. *Eur Heart J,* 30(21): 2606-13.

[55] Radi, S., Ostry, A., Lamontagne, A. D. (2007). Job stress and other working conditions: relationships with smoching behaviors in a representative sample of working Australians. *Am J Ind Med*, 50: 584-96.

[56] Rautaharju, P. M., Surawicz, B., Gettes, L. S., et al. (2009). AHA/ACCF/HRS Recommendations for the Standardization and Interpretation of the Electrocardiogram: Part IV: The ST Segment, T and U Waves, and the QT Interval A Scientific Statement From the American Heart Association Electrocardiography and Arrhythmias Committee, Council on Clinical Cardiology; the American College of Cardiology Foundation; and the Heart Rhythm Society Endorsed by the International Society for Computerized Electrocardiology. *J Am Coll Cardiol*, 53: 982-91.

[57] Ribas-Latre, A., Eckel-Mahan, K. (2016). Interdependence of nutrient metabolism and the circadian clock system: Importance for metabolic health. *Mol Metab*, 5(3): 133-52.

[58] Riva, M. M., Santini, M., Borleri, D., et al. (2016). Diabetes mellitus in critical jobs. *Med Lav*, 107(4): 293-9.

[59] Rotenberg, L., Silva-Costa, A., Vasconcellos-Silva P. R., et al. (2016). Work schedule and self-reported hypertension – the potential beneficial role of on-shift naps for night workers. *Chronobiol Int*, 33(6): 697-705.

[60] Sandi, C., Haller, J. (2015). Stress and the social brain: behavioral effects and neurobiological mechanisms. *Nat Rev Neurosci*, 16(5): 290-304.

[61] Silva-Costa, A., Rotenberg, L., Coeli, C. M., et al. (2016). Night work is associated with glycemic levels and anthropometric alterations preceding diabetes: Baseline results from ELSA-Brasil. *Chronobiol Int*, 33(1): 64-72.

[62] Shrestha, N., Pedisic, Z., Neil-Sztramko, S., et al. (2016). The impact of obesity in the workplace: a review of contributing factors, consequences and potential solutions. *Curr Obes Rep*, 2016, Jul 22. (Epub ahead of print).

[63] Son, M., Ye, B. J., Kim, J. I., et al. (2015). Association between shift work and obesity according to body fat percentage in Korean wage workers: data from the fourth and the fifth Korea National Health and Nutrition Examination Survey (KNHANES 2008-2011). *Ann Occup Environ Med*, 27: 32.

[64] Suessenbacher, A., Potocnik, M., Dorler, J., et al. (2011). Comparison of peripheral endothelial function in shift versus nonshift workers. *Am J Cardiol*, 107: 945-8.

[65] Suwazono, Y., Sakata, K., Okubo, Y., et al. (2006). Long-term longitudinal study on the relationship between alternating shift work and the onset of diabetes mellitus in male Japanese workers. *J Occup Environ Med*, 48(5): 455-61.

[66] Steptoe A. (2009). Night shift work and the cardiovascular health of medical staff. *Eur Heart J*, 30: 2560-1.

[67] Theorell, T., Akerstedt, E. (1976). Day and night work: changes in cholesterol, uric acid, glucose and potassium in serum and circadian patterns of urinary catecholamine excretion. *Acta Med Scand*, 200: 47-53.

[68] Yanagita, S., Amemlya, S., Suzuki, S., et al. (2007). Effects of spontaneous and forced running on activation of hypothalamic corticotropin-releasing hormone neurons in rats. *Life Sci*, 80(4): 356-63.

[69] Ye, H. H., Jeong, J. U., Jeon, M. J., et al. (2013). The association between shift work and the metabolic syndrome in female workers. *Ann Occup Environ Med*, 25: 33.

[70] Yoon, C. G., Kang, M. Y., Bae, K. J., et al. (2016). Do working hours and type of work affect obesity in South Korean Female Workers? Analysis of the Korean Community Health Survey. *J Womens Health (Larchmt)*, 25(2): 173-80.

[71] Yoshioka, E., Saijo, Y., Kita, T., et al. (2011). Relation between self-reported sleep duration and arterial stiffness: a cross-sectional study of middle-aged Japanese civil servants. *Sleep*, 34(12): 1681-6.

[72] Yu, E., Rimm, E., Qi, L., et al. (2016). Diet, lifestyle, biomarkers, genetic factors, and risk of cardiovascular disease in the nurses' health studies. *Am J Public Health*, 2016, Jul 26: e1-e8.

[73] Van Amelsvoort, L. G., Jansen, N. W., Kant, I. (2006). Smoking among shift workers: More than a confounding factor. *Chronobiol Int*, 23(6): 1105-13.

[74] Van Amelsvoort, L. G., Schouten, E. G., Maan, A. C., et al. (2001). Changes in frequency of premature complexes and heart rate variability related to shift work. *Occup Environ Med*, 58(10): 678-81.
[75] Van Amelsvoort, L. G., Schouten, E. G., Kok, F. J. (1999). Duration of shiftwork related to body mass index and waist to hip ratio. *Int J Obes Relat Metab Disord*, 23: 973-8.
[76] Vetter, C., Devore, E. E., Wegrzyn, L. R., et al. (2016). Association between rotating night shift work and risk of coronary heart disease among women. *JAMA*, 315(16): 1726-34.
[77] Wang, A., Arah, O. A., Kauhanen, J., et al. (2016). Shift work and 20-year incidence of acute myocardial infarction: results from the Kuopio ischemic heart disease risk factor study. *Occup Environ Med*, 2016, Mar 31. Pii: oemed-2015-103245. doi: 10.1136/oemed-2015-103245.
[78] Wolff, B., Völzke, H., Schwahn, C., et al. (2008). Relation of self-reported sleep duration with carotid intima-media thickness in a general population sample. *Atherosclerosis*, 196(2): 727-32.
[79] Zhao, Z., Yuan, Z., Ji, Y., et al. (2010). Left ventricular hypertrophy amplifies the QT, and Tp-e intervals and the Tp-e/QT ratio of the left chest ECG. *J Biomed Res*, 24: 69-72.

BIOGRAPHICAL SKETCH

Ioana Mozos

Affiliation: "Victor Babes" University of Medicine and Pharmacy, Timisoara, Romania, Department of Functional Sciences, Discipline of Pathophysiology

Education: MD, PhD

Research and Professional Experience:
Professional Appointments: Associate Professor, "Victor Babes" University of Medicine and Pharmacy, Timisoara, Romania, Department of Functional Sciences, Discipline of Pathophysiology

Honors: Price of the Romanian Society of Cardiology for Excellence in Research in Cardiology, 2013

Publications Last Three Years (Selection):

Mozos I. Links between serum uric acid level, blood pressure and QT interval in the general population, *Jokull*, 2016, 66: 79-90

Merlo S., Letonja M. S., Vujkovac A. C., Delev D., Mozos I., Kruzliak P., Petrovic D. Arachidonate 5-lipoxygenase (ALOX5) gene polymorphism (rs12762303) and arachidonate 5-lipoxygenase activating protein (ALOX5AP) gene plymorphism (rs3802278) and markers of carotid atherosclerosis in patients with type 2 diabetes mellitus. *Int J Clin Exp Med*, 2016, 9(2): 4509-14

Mozos I. Gligor S. Blood pressure variables, arterial stiffness, endothelial function and arterial age in sedentary and physically active smokers. *Jokull*, 2015, 65(12): 61-71

Mozos I., Mihaescu R. Pulse wave velocity and central hemodynamic indices in patients with malignant solid tumors *Jokull*, 2015, 65(12): 200-14

Mozos I., Mihaescu R. Crosstalk between arterial stiffness, arterial age and blood count in hematologic malignancies. *Jokull*, 2015, 65(9): 105-15

Mozos I., Caraba A. Electrocardiographic predictors of cardiovascular mortality *Dis Markers*, 2015, 727401. doi:10.1155/2015/727401

Mozos I., Marginean O. Links between Vitamin D Deficiency and Cardiovascular Diseases *BioMed Research International*, 2015, Article ID 109275

Mozos I. Mechanisms linking Red Blood Cell Disorders and Cardiovascular Diseases. *BioMed Research International*, 2015, Article ID 682054

Mozos I. The link between ventricular repolarization variables and arterial function. *J Electrocardiol*, 2015, 48(2): 145-9

Mozos I. Laboratory Markers of Ventricular Arrhythmia Risk in Renal Failure. *BioMed Research International*, 2014, Article ID 509204

Mozos I., Filimon L. QT and Tpeak-Tend intervals in shift workers. *J Electrocardiol*, 2013, 46 (1): 60-5

Mozos I., Filimon L. Arterial age and shift work. *Int J Collab Res Int Med Pub Health*, 2013, 5(5): 340-7.

In: Shift Work
Editors: Wan He and Lili Yu

ISBN: 978-1-53612-460-6
© 2017 Nova Science Publishers, Inc.

Chapter 3

ADAPTATION TO SHIFT WORK: THE ROLE OF AN ORGANIZATIONAL CONTEXT

Isabel S. Silva[*] *and Joana Prata*
School of Psychology, University of Minho, Braga, Portugal

ABSTRACT

Shift work, especially when performed during the night, has been associated with several negative consequences from the point of view of occupational health and safety (e.g., sleep and digestive problems, fatigue, work accidents). This work schedule can also have negative impacts on social life and workers' families, especially when working time collides with socially valued periods (e.g., Sunday, end of the day).

In order to minimize such consequences, several intervention strategies have been proposed, some focused on the worker himself, others on the organization. This chapter intends to present and reflect on the key strategies that can be implemented in an organizational context in order to promote adaptation to shift work. Specifically, it aims to promote the following strategies: design of shift systems, training and information provided by the organization to employees, possibility of holding naps at work, physical resources (e.g., canteen, transport), and working time management practices in terms of human resources (e.g., degree of involvement given to workers regarding the management of their working time). Regarding this last strategy (management practices of working time), the results of empirical studies carried out in Portugal, especially in

[*] Corresponding Author Email: isilva@psi.uminho.pt.

the industrial sector, will also be presented, where the relationship between the adoption of such practices and some of the effects typically associated with shift work, namely the ones regarding health and social effects, were analyzed. Anchored in this presentation, the conceptualization and operationalization of such organizational intervention strategy will also be discussed.

Keywords: shift work, shift systems, napping, training, human resource management

INTRODUCTION

The twenty-first century could be defined as the century of change. Change occurs on a regular basis in all aspects of our daily routines, whether it's political, economical, technological, social, etc. In order to be successful, organizations have to define their strategies to keep on up with these changes.

One of the main challenges organizations face has to do with working time arrangements. Working time arrangements that differ from the conventional one (i.e., 9:00 am - 5:00 pm, from Monday to Friday) have been increasing, including shift work. For example, according to the Fifth European Working Conditions Survey, in 2012, 19% of the active population of the European Union worked the night shift and 17% worked shift work (Eurofound, 2012). In 2015, the sixth edition of the same survey pointed out, on the other hand, that 19% realized night shifts and 21% shift work (Eurofound, 2015).

Shift work can be defined as "the way of organization of daily working hours in which different teams work in succession to cover more or all of the 24 h" (Costa, 1997, p. 89). This kind of working time arrangement can be found in several sectors (e.g., health, security, civil protection, chemical industry, auto industry, transport) (e.g., Boisard, Cartron, Gollac & Valeyre, 2003), and its implementation can allow operation for up to 24 hours a day, 365 days per year.

In general, the organization of working time in shifts, especially if it involves the night shift (that requires the inversion of the sleep-wake cycle) and highly valued periods from a social point of view, can represent, in comparison with fixed daytime schedules, added difficulties from the physiological and psychosocial perspective to the worker (Smith, Folkard & Fuller, 2003; Silva, 2012). On the other hand, the management of these schedules can equally add challenges to the organizations, in particular on the level of performance management, of safety (Folkard & Tucker, 2003) and of human resources (Silva & Prata, 2015).

Many researchers have tried to identify which factors can influence the adaptation to shift work in order to support interventions in a problematic scope. For example, according to Pisarski, Lawrence, Bohle & Brook (2008), there are six factors that play a crucial role in the adaptation to shift work: support from colleagues; work-life balance; team identity; team climate; control over the working environment; and support from supervisors, which proved to exercise the greatest influence. Nachreiner (1998) divides the diverse range of variables likely to influence adaptation to shift work in two groups: individual and situational nature. In general, it can be said that the scientific community is giving more attention to the variables included in the first group. For example, little attention has been paid to macro-level factors that interfere with shift work, like job design (Dollard, Osborne, & Manning, 2013) or domestic and social factors (Smith et al., 2003).

This chapter intends to present and reflect on the key strategies that can be implemented in an organizational context in order to promote adaptation to shift work. Specifically, it aims to promote the following strategies: design of shift systems, training and information provided by the organization to employees, possibility of holding naps at work, physical resources, and working time management practices in terms of human resources. Regarding this last strategy, the results of empirical studies carried out in Portugal will also be presented, where the relationship between the adoption of such practices and some of the effects typically associated with shift work, namely regarding health and social effects, were analyzed. Anchoring this presentation, the conceptualization and operationalization of such organizational intervention strategy will also be discussed.

ORGANIZATIONAL FACTORS THAT CAN PROMOTE SHIFT WORK ADAPTATION

Design of Shift Systems

Within the organizational factors that influence shift work adaptation, the design of shift systems is one of the most studied variables (Smith et al., 2003). There are thousands of different shift schedules which may have quite a different impact on workers' health and safety. Therefore, shift schedules should be designed according to some ergonomic criteria or characteristics (see, for example, Knauth, 1997 and Dall'Ora, Ball, Recio-Saucedo, & Griffiths, 2016), recognized to be suitable to lessen stress and limit adverse effects on health, well-being, and performance.

There is no magic formula in the design of a shift that works well for all workers and all organizations, since it involves many variables, for which there is some controversy. According to the European legislation, Council Directive 93/104/EU

> "every worker in the European Community shall have a right to a weekly rest period and to annual paid leave, the duration of which must be progressively harmonized in accordance with national practices". The same directive points out that "The Member States shall take the measures necessary to ensure that every worker is entitled to a minimum daily rest period of 11 consecutive hours per 24-hour period" and that "the average working time for each seven-day period, including overtime, does not exceed 48 hours."

These standards have been defined based on research documented in the literature. Its failure may involve human risks and materials, endangering not only the worker himself but also others, like the case, for example, of health care. Although the necessity in some organizations is a 24-hour operation period, much research has shown that the shifts that include night work - due to the circadian system - are those most difficult to adjust to (Monk, 1988). As such, one recommendation is, for example, that if night shifts are unavoidable due to operational needs, an appropriate level of staffing could minimize the number of overnight shifts required as far as possible while meeting the operational needs of the organizations.

Systems may differ in various characteristics (see, for example, Costa, 1997 or Thierry & Jansen, 1998). Among the different characteristics of shift systems those which have been highlighted in the literature review are: the rotation speed (number of days on each turn); the direction of rotation (is the direction of clockwise, or counterclockwise); length of shifts, which can vary by the number of days and the daily duration of each shift. These working arrangements may also vary in terms of whether they are fixed - when workers are always on the same shift - or rotating. There is also variability in the duration per day per month, pauses, and clearances, and in the case of rotating shifts, if these changes are in a clockwise sequence, or vice versa, as well as the speed of change.

In a recent literature review carried out by Dall'Ora et al., (2016) that was comprised of 35 studies (25 on the health sector) it was pointed out that the characteristics of shift work which play a greater role on workers' performance and well-being are: shift length; weekly hours; compressed work week; overtime; night work; and rest opportunities. Next, we will detail some of these characteristics.

Shift length is a characteristic widely investigated among different occupational sectors, the results being controversial (Ferguson & Dawson, 2012; Dall'Ora et al., 2016). The main discussion (and research) is between 8-hour shifts versus 12-hour shifts (e.g., Dall'Ora et al., 2016; Johnson & Sharit, 2001; Lowden, Kecklund, Axelsson & Åkerstedt, 1998; Mitchell & Williamson, 2000; Smith, Macdonald, Folkard & Tucker, 1998). According to some authors (e.g., Dall'Ora et al., 2016), an extended shift might have the advantage of fewer consecutive night shifts and longer blocks of time off. However, when the shifts are too long (≥12 hours), negative effects are registered on employees' performance, satisfaction and health, such as additional fatigue and sleep problems (Smith et al., 1998). In a study carried out by Stimpfel, Brewer and Kovner (2015) with 1744 newly licensed registered nurses from 34 US states, 12-hour (or longer) shifts were associated with an increased risk of a sprain or strain injury in comparison with shorter shifts. It is also important to notice that, as Merkus and colleagues observed on a study of self-reported recovery from 2-week 12-hour shift work schedules in 2015, the negative effects of long shifts - especially in terms of sleep quality - are more prevalent when the shift includes night work. Taking these results into consideration, the physical and mental load of the task should be taken into account by organizations when considering the length of a work shift.

Overall, it seems that there isn't data that allows stating that the 8-hour shift is preferable to the 12-hour shift or vice versa. Despite the absence of a correct answer to this question, the evidence alerts us to the importance of monitoring the adaptation to shift work over time, mostly because the negative effects that result from shift work might take time to be noticed (Dall'Ora et al., 2016); frequently when starting a new job, workers suffer from the so called "honeymoon effect" (Dwyer, Jamieson, Moxham, Austen & Smith, 2007).

In conclusion, there are some recommendations the authors provide regarding shift length. Unless justified by special circumstances, such as important operational requirements or a preference generally shared by the staff concerned, unduly extended shift (including overtime) should be avoided as far as practicable (e.g., Smith et al., 2003; Dwyer et al., 2007). If the work is continuous throughout a shift and is also demanding, monotonous, dangerous and safety-critical, employers should consider whether shortening each shift is necessary, or should consider introducing rest breaks - this topic will be developed further - in each shift to help employees cope with their work mentally and physically (e.g., Dall'Ora et al., 2016; Knauth, 1993; Lowden et al., 1998; Smith et al., 1998).

Despite limited evidence regarding weekly hours, most of the studies on this matter concluded that more than 40 weekly hours of shift work may result in a negative impact on an employee's health, performance and job satisfaction, which meets the recommendations of the labor law of most countries (Directive, 2003/08/EC, 2003). According to the recent literature review provided by Dall'Ora et al. (2016), a recent study conducted in the US with more than 11,500 nurses showed that the nurses who worked more than 40 weekly hours of shift work in comparison with the ones working 30 - 40 hours per week had an increased risk of error (e.g., patient falls with injury; medication errors). In another study with 7013 workers, Artazcoz, Cortès, Escribà-Agüir, Cascant and Villegas (2009) verified that in men, working 50 - 60 hours per week was associated with job dissatisfaction in comparison with those working 30 - 40 hours per week. Another study focusing on organizational climate and hospital nurses' caring practices concluded that the workload leads to a decreased performance and neglect of caring practices (Roch, Dubbois, & Clarke, 2014).

Regarding the beginning of the shift, in the case of morning shifts, the evidence indicates that the shift should not start too early because the earlier the morning shift starts, the higher the probability of sleeping less (e.g., Costa, 2010; Knauth, 1997). Early morning shifts may be associated with shorter sleep and greater fatigue (e.g., Kecklund, Åkerstedt, & Lowden, 1997). It is advisable to avoid early morning starts as far as practicable and consider fitting the shift time in with the availability of transport, in particular for workplaces in remote locations and with employees having to travel for long hours to work (e.g., Knauth, 1996; Pilcher, Lambert, & Huffcutt, 2000; Postnova, Robinson, & Postnov, 2013). Regarding the night shift, Postnova et al.'s (2013) results showed that scheduling of such shifts to start at 9:00 pm instead of 12:00 am reduces sleep drive.

In the case of rotating shifts, the literature generally recommend a "forward rotating shift" pattern, in the order of early shift, late shift and night shift. Some studies have shown that a "forward rotating shift," that is, the rotation in a clockwise direction (also known as a phase delay) facilitates adaptation, in particular regarding sleep (e.g., Folkard, 1992; Knauth, 1996, 1997; Smith et al., 2003). The main argument that supports these findings has to do with the fact that the biological clock adjusts better when moving ahead than back (Barton & Folkard, 1993; Knauth, 1996; Smith et al., 2003). In general, empirical studies (e.g., Amelsvoort, Jansen, Swaen, van den Brandt, & Kant, 2004; Barton & Folkard, 1993; Lavie, Tzischinsky, Epstein, & Zomer, 1992; Tucker, Smith, & Folkard., 2000) have given support to this recommendation, though the "backward rotating system" is frequently used in organizations (e.g., Amelsvoort et al., 2004) and also presents an advantage from the point of view of the workers (see, for example, Åkerstedt, 2003). It is also important to attend to the transition between shifts, it being recommended, in a general way (e.g., Knauth, 1997) to avoid quick changes between shifts so as not to compromise the time dedicated to rest. As concluded by Dall'Ora et al. (2016), quick returns between shifts seem to be related to an increase in tiredness. Beyond the previous considerations, as regards Costa (2010), it is essential to keep the shift system as regular as possible.

In terms of the rotation of shifts, organizations should also take into account when designing the shift the length of the rotation period (e.g., the number of days on anyone's shifts before switching to the next shift). In this context, the issue that is perhaps the most debated in the scientific community is connected with the number of successive nights of work (i.e., fixed shifts versus rotating systems), there not being a consensus about all aspects of this issue. For example, a recent review of Dall'Ora et al. (2016) concluded that while the rotating systems (evolving nights) are associated with a poorer performance, the night fixed shift is associated with an increased dissatisfaction in workers.

Another thing organizations should take into consideration regarding shift design is rest break arrangements. Suitable rest breaks for employees allow them to relax and recuperate. This is particularly important for employees working in shifts, especially rotating shifts. Apart from rest breaks within a shift, there should also be time for rest between shifts. Many studies have shown that breaks and rest opportunities can benefit employees in terms of fatigue and alertness (e.g., Dall'Ora et al., 2016; Pilcher et al., 2000). However, there isn't enough data to determine the quality these rest breaks should have in order to have this positive impact (Dall'Ora et al., 2016). In a study carried out by Lee et al. (2016) regarding the high risk of near-crash driving events following night-shift work, there was increasing drowsiness and impaired driving performance despite the breaks.

Although some authors suggest that the impact of shift work characteristics on outcomes is likely to be occupation specific (Ferguson & Dawson, 2012), Dall'Ora et al.'s (2016) results suggest that there is no significant difference by occupational sector. In conclusion, Knauth (1997) inferred there might not be a perfect shift system which can be recommended for all kinds of work. Nevertheless, there are more favorable and less favorable systems, and organizations should try to design the shiftwork systems the best they can, trying as much as possible to take into account the individual needs of workers. This also requires the workers' participation in the whole process of designing and implementing the shift schedules, not only because of their direct experience of the problems, but also to promote good motivation for adopting the most convenient coping strategies that are able to limit, as much as possible, significant perturbations of their health and social life (Costa, 2010).

Napping

The practice of napping by shift workers in order to compensate for the reduction of sleep is a frequent practice in association with the night shift or with the morning shift with a very early start (Åkerstedt, 2003; Kecklund et al., 1997). The review by Åkerstedt (2003) indicated that about a third of workers assigned to those shifts have this behavior.

From the previous description, the practice of napping is made outside the organizational context. However, due to the advantages associated with this strategy in the management of vigilance levels and tiredness during night work (e.g., Åkerstedt & Landström, 1998; Åkerstedt, 2003; Bonnefond et al., 2001), its realization is also recommended in the workplace (e.g., Estryn-Behar et al., 2012). Despite the advantages associated with this practice, its acceptance by workers is not so obvious (Bonnefond et al., 2001), and it may also have barriers to its implementation from enterprises and occupational contexts (Fallis, McMillan, & Edwards, 2011). In any case, as per Kogi (2000), it has witnessed the growth of the formal possibility of napping practices in other countries, besides Japan.

The recommendation of realizing a sleeping period in the workplace is not, however, free of inconvenience. In fact, a potential disadvantage is sleep inertia, which may impoverish the performance on the following period after waking, as alertness levels may be decreased during this period (Kogi, 2000; Fallis et al., 2011). Therefore, the time frame available for realizing napping in the workplace should take into account this phenomenon, and must, according to Åkerstedt (2003), contemplate a period between five and fifteen minutes for this purpose.

Both studies that we will next describe, one in the industrial context and the other in the health context, we believe help to illustrate the main benefits and the main barriers or difficulties associated with the implementation of this strategy in a real context.

The study of Bonnefond et al. (2001) evaluated the implementation of a napping practice in the workplace with 12 workers of a French industrial company throughout the course of a year. All the workers were men who worked on a quick rotation shift system and were experienced in the shift work regime. The night shift hours were from 8:45 pm until 6:00 am, and the workers could use a reserved area for breaking or napping for up to one hour during the period between 11:30 pm and 3:30 am. In the results, it was noticed that the execution of a short rest period occurs in over 50% of the night shifts, with an average throughout the year of 67%. On the other hand, the mean frequency of occurrence of these episodes when the workers slept was 77.5% and this rate was very stable over the year. The average duration of napping estimated for the workers was about 30 minutes. It was also observed that the implementation of the strategy was associated with general satisfaction with the quality and the facility of the night shift, as the surveillance level was considered higher on the following hours after the napping. Throughout that time an improvement was also observed in the adaptation process to the available strategy. Indeed, after a half year, two-thirds of the workers considered themselves "very well adapted" to the new organization of the night shift. Therefore, at the time there was an increase in satisfaction levels, as in the last four months of the study, over half of the persons declared themselves "totally satisfied" with the possibility of enjoying a "short time to rest". In the matter of the disadvantages associated with the practice of napping in the workplace, the workers mentioned the delayed bedtime ("loss of will to sleep") after the work shift. In any case, it is of concern that in the first semester of the study, two-thirds of workers reported a decrease in their desire to go to bed, although in more than 80% of cases, this reduction stabilized during the second semester.

More recently, Fallis et al. (2011) sought to find out nurses' practices, preferences and perceptions of napping/not napping when they were working the night shift and with the benefits and drawbacks associated with such

In total, 13 professionals were interviewed (11 women and two men), of which 54% were aged between 31 and 50 years. Nine worked in the emergency department and four on an intensive care unit of a Canadian hospital. Notice that the hospital didn't have a written policy about napping on breaks. Ten of the thirteen professionals (77%) mentioned that every time that occupational circumstances allowed (e.g., staffing level), they took a nap during the shift, and its duration varied. The workers that mentioned they take a nap regularly identified the advantages of this practice as an improvement of humor, the capacity for judgment, and feeling refreshed or energized. As for the three professionals that didn't take a nap, two of them mentioned that they felt disoriented after this practice, and that is the reason why they didn't adopt it. Given this fear (sleep inertia), the authors conclude that the recovery period after the napping can be a critical component of the planning strategy, a recommendation, by the way, also made by other authors (e.g., Åkerstedt, 2003). Still, on the results level of this study, the workers mentioned several reasons why they aren't able to nap. Among the reasons, beyond the fear of sleep inertia, we also highlight the lack of a comfortable place for this purpose to avoid interruptions during rest/sleep and the perception that management didn't support this behavior.

Resources Provided

As described in the previous section, the absence of a place itself and of comfort was identified by the nurses of the Fallis et al. study (2011) as a barrier for don't to realizing napping in the workplace. Beyond the physical resources available (not just for the napping, but also for rest), the organizations might provide another type of physical resources to promote and facilitate the adaptation to shift work. Specifically, they can offer information and advice services (a strategy that will be discussed in the next section), access to hot meals and access to transport.

Providing similar facilities on different shifts offers a familiar environment, which could better enable employees to cope with shift work. It is important to have a canteen or cafeteria that provides hot meals and is open all day. This is especially important during the night shift, which might lack access to good meals that are necessary in order to have more energy and fight fatigue (Monk & Folkard, 1992). In this context, the revision of Åkerstedt and Landström (1998) concludes that the moderate consumption of caffeine and napping are the most efficient strategies to deal with somnolence during the night work period.

In terms of the mode of transportation, many studies revealed an increased risk of accident, especially when leaving a night shift (see, for example, Lee et al., 2015), so it would be good if the organization could provide a collective means of transportation. As an alternative, employees may use public transport rather than driving to and from work and could avoid tiredness from driving before and after undertaking shift work, but in this case, there is a time limitation since there isn't public transportation at all times during the day. The resources that the community offers, in this case, a transportation schedule, might also constitute an important aspect of facilitating work in non-standard work schedules.

In terms of facilities, Monk and Folkard (1992) also refer to the importance of having a recreational space in which employees can get along and rest. For their part, Pagnan, Lero and MacDermid Wadsworth (2011), present some strategies to reduce the family-work conflict in the shift work context. Specifically, they suggest the possibility of parents having access to a cell phone to maintain contact with their children, in particular during the night shift, an enlargement of the break during the shift system to allow parents to go home at meal time or at kids' bedtimes and availability of a leisure area to receive the family during working breaks.

As described in this section, companies can provide physical resources to promote and facilitate adaptation to shift work, especially for the night shift. However, it is necessary to evaluate the efficiency of these possibilities of intervention given the shortage of literature available on this matter.

Information/Advising

The provision of information, advising or training of workers to help deal with the difficulties related to shift work (e.g., sleep) is another strategy discussed in the literature (e.g., Dhande & Sharma, 2011; Härmä & Ilmarinen, 1999; Knauth & Horneberg, 2003). In this context, Knauth and Horneberg (2003) also refer to the fact that some managers don't have direct experience with shift work or knowledge about potential problems and possible intervention strategies. If we also understand that some of the trouble experienced by those that work on shifts are related to the family-work interface (e.g., Demerouti, Geurts, & Bakker, 2004; Mauno, Ruokolainen & Kinnunen, 2015; Tuttle & Garr, 2012), the families of those who do shift work constitute a target potential of this type of intervention, so that they may be sensitized to the problems that employees may feel and learn possible ways of minimizing problems in the familial context.

Therefore, with the purpose of transmitting knowledge and recommendations that can help with shift work adaptation, informational material is being developed, including periodical publications (e.g., Wedderburn, 1991) and manuals, mainly directed at shift workers (e.g., Monk & Folkard, 1992; Shapiro, Heslegrave, Beyers, & Picard, 1997). In a general way, these materials focus on the main problems that shift workers may experience, strategies to handle those difficulties and information about biological clocks and the circadian system. For example, the manual developed by Shapiro et al. (1997) entitled "Working the shift: A self-health guide" is structured on five parts or themes: "Understanding your body clock," "Clocks in collision", "How to cope with shift work," "The shift working for family" and "The shift working workplace."

To ensure the relevance and accuracy of recommendations available on different topics (e.g., sleep, feeding, management of alert levels, physical exercises) the necessity of testing these recommendations in the field through well-controlled studies has been highlighted (e.g., Wedderburn, 1993; Wedderburn & Scholarios, 1993). Indeed, the evaluation of the effectiveness of this strategy type, that is, information provision, either by manual delivery or using other formats such as workshops and training, is rather scarce (Rankin & Wedderburn, 2000). In any case, some of the available studies (e.g., Smith-Coggins, Rosekind, Buccino, Dibges, & Moser, 1997; Rankin & Wedderburn, 2000) have shown that the obtained results, at best, are quite modest. In this context Tepas (1993) also highlights that if the target is to promote changes in the shift worker's behavior in the long-term, it's necessary to provide the resource of training programs, since the mere disclosure of information is of limited use. In addition, these training programs must be based on the evaluation of the necessities of a given context and should be the assessment target if they intend to maximize strategy efficiency.

The provision of information and advice to workers can be made, however, from other professionals in (e.g., occupational medicine) or outside the organization (e.g., family medicine) and informally (Silva & Prata, 2015). For example, in the Silva (2008) study, was interviewed several organizational actors (e.g., occupational physician and nurse, human resources managers, administration) of five Portuguese textile companies about their perceptions of difficulties related to shift work, as the strategies eventually adopted by the organization were meant to deal with them. Although none of the organizations were formally offered any information or advising about shift work, it was noticed that the occupational physician professionals were able to provide some information, mainly related to sleep, when there were regular medical surveillance consultations in the company. Given the above, we believe that the proper training and awareness that these professionals may give regarding shift work is essential, including the human resource managers and supervisors as we shall see in the following section.

Human Resource Management Practices

In the recommendations of several authors (e.g., Costa, 2010; Dhande & Sharma, 2011; Demerouti et al., 2004; Härmä & Ilmarinen, 1999; Estryn-Béhar et al., 2012; Jeppesen & Boggild, 2000; Knauth & Hornberger, 2003; Šimunic & Gregov, 2012), in order to promote tolerance of shift work, the importance of having flexibility and participation by workers is frequently referenced. For example, Demerouti et al., (2004) propose that the shift systems that involve rotation should be drawn with a high level of individualization and flexibility, and Knauth and Hornberger (2003) highlight the importance of a participative approach to the reformulation and implementation of the shift system. Indeed, the possibility of influence by the worker on aspects related to his working time may manifest itself in several scenarios, as with the (re)design of the shift systems, the possibility of choice of a given schedule or on the possibility of changes between shifts (Jeppesen, & Boggild, 2000; Pisarski, Bohle, & Callan, 1998, 2002; Silva & Prata, 2015).

The organizations differ on the degree of involvement that workers are allowed with regards to different aspects of their work. For example, in the Silva (2008) study to which we have already referred, in some textile companies a high concern was observed in involving the workers (e.g., shift choice in admission, facilitating exchanges between shifts); in others, this concern was apparently absent from the human resources management practices.

It's expected that the availability of flexible practices of working time within organizations will allow a better adjustment to the workers' needs and increase their sense of control over their working hours. Although the empirical literature that relates organizational working time management and tolerance for shift work practices is scarce, there is evidence that supports the importance of the control perception variable in understanding the effects associated with shift work and night work (e.g., Barton, 1994; Pisarski et al.,

1998). If we consider that the individual characteristics (e.g., age, chronotype) can influence tolerance to shift work, and the circumstances of shift workers can vary considerably throughout the life cycle (e.g., household structure), enjoyment of a certain flexibility provided by the organizational context certainly will make the adjustments easier that will eventually be found necessary. As discussed in Silva, Prata and Ferreira (2014), the strategy of flexibility from the point of view of human resources management is doubly advantageous: if, on the one hand, it allows organizations to accommodate differences more easily between workers from a situational perspective (e.g., conciliation with school schedules of children; spouse working hours), on the other hand, it also makes it easier to accommodate differences in the individual/biological domain with regards to shifts available (e.g., Morningness-Eveningness, that is, personal preferences to perform activities/ rest during 24-hour period).

Still, with regards to support on the organizational context level, the supervisors, and working colleagues may perform an important role. For example, in the Pisarski et al., study (1998), with nurses working on rotating shifts, direct and indirect effects of the support of colleagues and supervisors were observed in terms of the conflict of work/non-work life and psychological health. On the other hand, it was observed that the social support of the supervisor on the conflict of work/non-work was mediated by the control that the shift workers could have on their matches/assignments to shifts. In this context, it was also noted that the literature on family-friendly practices (e.g., Mills, Matthews, Henning, & Woo, 2014) has drawn attention to the role that organizations can play in the management of the interface of work and family, not only through formal practices, but also through the development of an organizational "family-friendly" culture, translated in the way supervisors manage this interface with the workers in everyday life. In the case of shift workers, such management/flexibility may pass, for example, by the authorization or not of exchanges between shifts.

In short, it seems that organizations might influence the process of adaptation to shift work with the type of working time management practices they adopt or not. We finish this section with the presentation of results from four studies conducted in the North of Portugal which sought to investigate this association. In all studies (cf., Table 1) effects typically associated with shift work through scales available in literature were evaluated (e.g., the Portuguese version of the Standard Shiftwork Index of Barton et al., 1995, for the evaluation of "digestive problems") or developed for the purpose (e.g., "satisfaction with the working time" scale developed by Silva, 2008). The number of scale items oscillated between three and seven, and in all cases Cronbach's alpha value was higher than 0.7.

Table 1. Correlation between the effects evaluated in each study and the perception of support of the organizational context related to the shifts in four studies realized in Portugal

Effects	Silva (2008) (N = 752) (textile industry)	Ferreira and Silva (2013) (N = 122) (textile industry)	Prata and Silva (2013) (N = 490) (electronic industry)	Silva and Silva (N = 52) (hospitality industry)
Sleep complaints	-.12**		-.27***	
Digestive complaints	-.15*		-.24***	
Psychological strength			.28***	
Interface working time/non work	.31**	.41***	.47***	.49**
Family life		.32*		
Conjugal life		.30**		
Working time satisfaction	.28**	.30**	.44***	.31*

*$p < .05$; ** $p < .01$; *** $p < .001$.

In each study, the dimension designated as the perception of organizational context support face to the shifts was also evaluated with a scale. This dimension aimed to assess the perceived support by workers in how the organization realizes "work management shift" or, if we will, regards human resource management practices for shift workers. Specifically, the scale sought to assess the perception of respondents regarding the organization's practices and concerns about the selection and placement of employees in shifts, responding to shift change requests, or how people's management is made when there is a need to reorganize shifts, including its concern with communication. In other words, they sought to evaluate how the organization shows that it is interested in promoting the adjustment between the preferences and individual needs of shift workers and organizational needs through certain resource management practices adopted.

This scale was developed by Silva (2008) from interviews with shift workers and various organizational actors (e.g., human resources managers) and literature (e.g., Eisenberger, Huntington, Hutchison, & Sowa, 1986). In its original version, the scale consists of four items, answered on a Likert 5-point scale from (1) strongly disagree to (5) totally agree. The four items are: i) *"The company does everything possible to place workers in the shifts they prefer"*; ii) *"As a rule, when workers need to change shifts the company responds favorably"*; iii) *"The company takes into account the situation of workers when it is necessary to have personnel changes between shifts*"; and iv) "*The company takes into account the workers' preferences for a particular shift when they are hired*". In one of the studies (Ferreira & Silva, 2013), the scale integrated one more item ("*Whenever it is necessary to change personnel between shifts, the company always informs the workers.*") while in another study (Prata & Silva, 2013), the third item previously mentioned was eliminated at the request of the company. The Cronbach's alpha was greater than .80 in all versions used.

On Table 1 there are the Pearson correlations between the perception of "support the organizational context related to the shifts" and the various effects evaluated in each study on the health level ("sleep complaints", "digestive complaints" and "psychological strength"), life outside the organization ("satisfaction with interface work/non-work", "family life" and "conjugal life") and "satisfaction with working time" in the respective samples of shift workers. In all cases, the associations go in the expected direction, that is, higher perception of organizational context of support, fewer health problems, greater satisfaction with working time arrangements and dimensions of social/family life. It was also observed that higher values tend to be associated with dimensions of a more social nature.

CONCLUSION

In this chapter, we present possibilities for intervention that can be adopted by organizations to promote adaptation to shift work. Of the strategies, those focused on shift system design have been the most studied by the scientific community and will virtually be the most effective given its focus on the "source" of the problem. Therefore, the need has been highlighted for more research in this area, mainly from longitudinal studies and well-controlled designs. On the other hand, as highlighted by Dall'Ora et al. (2016) the research focused on the characteristics of shifts tends to consider only one feature at a time, and does not integrate the underlying complexity of this schedule arrangement.

The role of the organizational context, however, is not limited to the design of the best shift system considering operational needs and the needs of workers in a given organization. As we have seen throughout this chapter, this can (and, in our perspective, should) go through the availability of resources, whether physical (e.g., refectory, suitable place for resting), informative/advising (e.g., coping strategies to deal with sleepiness during the night shift) and the adoption of flexible and participatory practices from the point of view of human resource management. In any case, regarding these intervention proposals, points from the literature need to be evaluated for their effectiveness.

The range of variables likely to influence tolerance to shift work are many and of varied types (Costa, 2003; Nachreiner, 1998; Saksvik, Bjorvatn, Hetland, Sandal, &Pallesen, 2010; Smith et al., 2003), covering individual characteristics to the community features where the organization is located. For example, Costa (2003) combines them into five categories: personal characteristics (e.g., age, gender); family and housing conditions (e.g., number and age of children); working conditions (e.g., work organization, compensation of payments); and social conditions (e.g., social support, transport). Given the above, other contexts (e.g., family, community, society) besides the organizational context also play a fundamental role in promoting or not this mode of organization of working time. In short, according to the range of variables involved, intervention in shift work will always require a multifaceted approach.

REFERENCES

Åkerstedt, T. (2003). Shift work and disturbed sleep/wakefulness. *Occupational Medicine, 53*, 89-94.

Åkerstedt, T., & Landström, U. (1998). Work place countermeasures of night fatigue. *International Journal of Industrial Ergonomics, 21*, 167-168.

Amelsvoort, L., Jansen, N., Swaen, G., van den Brandt, P., & Kant, J. (2004). Direction of shift rotation among three-shift workers in relation to psychological health and work-family conflict. Scandinavian *Journal of Work and Environmental Health, 30*(2), 149-156.

Artazcoz, L., Cortès, I., Escribà-Agüir, V., Cascant, L., & Villegas, R. (2009). Understanding the relationship of long working hours with health status and health-related behaviours. *Journal of Epidemiology Community Health, 63*(7), 521-527.

Barton, J. (1994). Choosing to work at night: A moderating influence on individual tolerance to shift work. *Journal of Applied Psychology, 79*(3), 449-454.

Barton, J., Spelten, E., Totterdell, P., Smith, L., Folkard, S., & Costa, G. (1995). The Standard Shiftwork Index: A battery of questionnaires for assessing shiftwork-related problems. *Work & Stress, 9*(1), pp. 4-30.

Barton, J., & Folkard, S. (1993). Advancing versus delaying shift systems. *Ergonomics, 36*(1-3), 59-64.

Boisard, P., Cartron, D., Gollac, M., & Valeyre, A. (2003). *Time and work: Duration of work*. Ireland: European Foundation for the Improvement of Living and Working Conditions.

Bonnefond, A., Muzet, A., Winter-Dill, A., Bailloeuil, C., Bitouze, F., & Bonneau, A. (2001). Innovative working schedule: Introducing one short nap during the night shift. *Ergonomics, 44*(10), 937-945.

Costa, G. (1997). The problem: Shiftwork. *Chronobiology International: The Journal of Biological and Medicine Rhythm Research, 13*(2), 89-98.

Costa, G. (2003). Factors influencing health of workers and tolerance to shift work. *Theory Issues in Ergonomic Science, 4*(3-4), 263-288.

Costa, G. (2010). Shift work and health: Current problems and preventive actions. *Safety and Health at Work, 1*(2), 112–123.

Dall'Ora, C., Ball, J., Recio-Saucedo, A., & Griffiths, P. (2016). Characteristics of shift work and their impact on employee performance and wellbeing: A literature review. *International Journal of Nursing Studies, 57*, 12-27.

Demerouti, E., Geurts, S. A., & Bakker, A. B. (2004). The impact of shiftwork on workhome conflict, job attitudes and health. *Ergonomics, 47*(9), 987-1002.

Dhande, K. K., & Sharma, S. (2011). Influence of shift work in process industry on workers' occupational health, productivity, and family and social life: An ergonomic approach. *Human Factors and Ergonomics in Manufactoring & Service Industries, 21*(3), 260-268.

Directive 93/104/EU. http://ec.europa.eu/social/main.jsp?catId = 706&langId = en&intPageId = 205.

Directive, 2003/08/EC. http://eur-lex.europa.eu/legal-content/EN/ALL/?uri = celex%3A32003L0044.

Dollard, M. F., Osborne, K., & Manning, I. (2013). Organization–environment adaptation: A macro-level shift in modeling work distress and morale. *Journal of Organizational Behavior, 34*(5), 629-647.

Dwyer, T., Jamieson, L., Moxham, L., Austen, D., & Smith, K. (2007). Evaluation of the 12-hour shift trial in a regional intensive care unit. *Journal of Nursing Management, 15*(7), 711-20.

Eisenberger, R., Huntington, R., Hutchison, S., & Sowa, D. (1986). Perceived organizational support. *Journal of Applied Psychology, 71*(3), 500-507.

Estryn-Behar, M., Van der Heijden, B., & the NEXT Study Group. (2012). Effects of extended work shifts on employee fatigue, health, satisfaction, work/family balance, and patient safety. *Work, 41*, 4283-4290.

European Foundation for the Improvement of Living and Working Conditions – Eurofound. (2012). *Fifth European Working Conditions Survey.* Luxembourg: Publications office of the European Union.

European Foundation for the Improvement of Living and Working Conditions – Eurofound. (2015). *First findings: Sixth European Working Conditions Survey.* Publications office of the European Union.

Fallis, W. M., McMillan, D. E., Edwards, M. P. (2011). Napping during night shift: Practices, preferences, and perceptions of critical care and emergency department nurses. *Critical Care Nurses, 31*(2), e1-e11.

Ferguson, S. A., & Dawson, D. (2012). 12-h or 8-h shifts? It depends. *Sleep Medicine Reviews, 16*(6), 519-528.

Ferreira, A. I., & Silva, I. S. (2013). Trabalho em turnos e dimensões sociais: Um estudo na indústria têxtil [Shiftwork and social dimensions: A study in the textile industry]. Estudos *de Psicologia, 18*(3), 477-485.

Folkard, S. (1992). Is there a 'best compromise' shift system? *Ergonomics, 35*(12), 1453-1463.

Folkard, S., & Tucker, P. (2003). Shift work, safety and productivity. *Occupational Medicine, 53*, 95-101.

Härmä, M., & Ilmarinen, J. E. (1999). Towards the 24-hour society – new approaches for aging shift workers? *Scandinavian Journal of Work and Environmental Health, 25*(6), 610-615.

Jeppesen, H. J., & Boggild, H. (2000). Redesigning shift schedules through a participatory intervention approach. In S. Hornberger, P. Knauth, G. Costa & S. Folkard (Eds.), *Shiftwork in the 21st century* (pp. 363-368). Frankfurt: Peter Lang.

Johnson, M. D., & Sharit, J. (2001). Impact of a change from an 8-h to a 12-h shift schedule on workers and occupational injury rates. *International Journal of Industrial Ergonomics, 27*, 303-319.

Kecklund, G., Åkerstedt, T., & Lowden, A. (1997). Morning work: Effects of early rising on sleep and alertness. *Sleep, 20*(3), 215-223.

Kogi, K. (2000). Should shiftworkers nap? Spread, roles and effects on-duty napping. In S. Hornberger, P. Knauth, G. Costa & S. Folkard (Eds.), *Shiftwork in the 21st century* (pp. 31-36). Frankfurt: Peter Lang.

Knauth, P. (1993). The design of shift systems. *Ergonomics, 36*(1-3), 15-28.

Knauth, P. (1996). Designing better shift systems. *Applied Ergonomics, 27*(1), 39-44.

Knauth, P. (1997). Changing schedules: Shiftwork. *Chronobiology International, 14*(2), 159-171.

Knauth, P., & Hornberger, S. (2003). Preventive and compensatory measures for shift workers. *Occupational Medicine, 53*, 109-116.

Lavie, P., Tzischinsky, O., Epstein, R., & Zomer, J. (1992). Sleep-wake cycle in shiftworkers on a "clockwise" and "counter-clockwise" rotation system. *Israel Journal of Medical Sciences, 28*(8-9), 636- 644.

Lee, M., L.; Howarda, M., E.; Horreyd, W., J.; Liangd, Y.; Andersona, C.; Shreevea, M. S. O'Briena, C. S., & Czeisler, C. A. (2016). High risk of near-crash driving events following night-shift work. *Proceedings of the National Academy of Sciences, 113*(1), 176–181.

Lowden, A., Kecklund, G., Axelsson, J., & Akersted, T. (1998). Change from an 8-hour shift, attitudes, sleep, sleepiness and performance. *Scandinavian Journal of Work and Environmental Health, 24*(Suppl. 3), 69-75.

Mauno, S., Ruokolainen, M., & Kinnunen, U. (2015). Work–family conflict and enrichment from the perspective of psychosocial resources: Comparing Finnish healthcare workers by working schedules. *Applied Ergonomics, 48*, 86-94.

Merkus, S. L., Holte, K. A, Huysmans, M. A., Ven, P. M., Mechelen, W., & Beek, A. J. (2015). Self-reported recovery from 2-week 12-hour shift work schedules: A 14-day follow-up. *Safety and Health at Work, 6*(3), 240–248.

Mills, M. J., Matthews, R. A., Henning, J. B., & Woo, V. A. (2014). Family-supportive organizations and supervisors: How do they influence employee outcomes and for whom?. *The International Journal of Human Resource Management, 25*(12), 1763-1785.

Mitchell, R. J., & Williamson, A. M. (2000). Evaluation of an 8 hour versus a 12 hour shift roster on employees at a power station. *Applied Ergonomics, 31*, 83-93.

Monk, T. H. (1988). Coping with the stress of shiftwork. *Work & Stress, 2*, 169-172.

Monk, T. H., & Folkard, S. (1992). *Making shiftwork tolerable.* London: Taylor & Francis.

Nachreiner, F. (1998). Individual and situational determinants of shiftwork tolerance. *Scandinavian Journal of Work and Environmental Health, 24*(Suppl. 3), 35-42.

Pagnan, C. E., Lero, D. S., & MacDermid Wadsworth, S. M. (2011). It doesn't always add up: examining dual-earner couples' decision to off-shift. *Community, Work & Family, 14*(3), 297-316.

Pilcher, J. J., Lambert, B. J., & Huffcutt, A. I. (2000). Differential effects of permanent and rotating shifts on self-report sleep length: A meta-analytic review. *Sleep*, *23*(2), k155-163.

Pisarski, A., Bohle, P., & Callan, V. J. (1998). Effects of coping strategies, social support and work-nonwork conflict on shift worker's health. *Scandinavian Journal of Work and Environmental Health*, *24*(Suppl. 3), 141-145.

Pisarski, A., Bohle, P., & Callan, V. J. (2002). Extended shifts in ambulance work: Influences on health. *Stress and Health*, *18*, 119-126.

Pisarski, A., Lawrence S. A., Bohle, P., & Brook, C. (2008). Organizational influences on the work life conflict and health of shiftworkers. *Applied Ergonomics*, *39*(5), 580-588.

Postnova, S., Robinson, P. A., & Postnov, D. D. (2013). Adaptation to shift work: Physiologically based modeling of the effects of lighting and shifts' start time. *PLoS ONE*, *8*(1), e53379.

Prata, J., & Silva, I. S. (2013). Efeitos do trabalho em turnos na saúde e em dimensões do contexto social e organizacional: Um estudo na indústria electrónica [Shiftwork effects on health and on social and organizational life: A study in the electronics industry]. *Revista Psicologia: Organizações e Trabalho*, *13*(2), 141-154.

Rankin, A., & Wedderburn, A. (2000). Evaluation of a shiftworkers guide. In S. Hornberger, P. Knauth, G. Costa & S. Folkard (Eds.), *Shiftwork in the 21st century* (pp. 405-410). Frankfurt: Peter Lang.

Roch, G., Dubois CA., & Clarke, S. P. (2014). Organizational climate and hospital nurses' caring practices: A mixed-methods study. *Research in Nursing & Health*, *37*(3), 229-40.

Saksvik, I., Bjorvatn, B., Hetland, H., Sandal., G., & Pallesen, S. (2010). Individual differences in tolerance to shift work – A systematic review. *Sleep Medicine*, *15*, 221-235.

Shapiro, C., Heslegrave, R., Beyers, J., & Picard, L. (1997). *Working the shift: A self-health guide*. JoliJoco Publications, Inc.

Silva, I. S. (2008). *Adaptação ao trabalho por turnos* [Adaptation to shift work]. Dissertação de Doutoramento em Psicologia do Trabalho e das Organizações [PhD in Work and Organizational Psychology]. Braga: Universidade do Minho.

Silva, I. S. (2012), *As condições de trabalho no trabalho por turnos. Conceitos, efeitos e intervenções [The working conditions in shift work. Concepts, effects and interventions]*, Climepsi Editores, Lisboa.

Silva, I. S., Prata, J., & Ferreira, A. I. (2014). Horários de trabalho por turnos: Da avaliação dos efeitos às possibilidades de intervenção [Shiftwork schedules: From effect's evaluation to intervention possibilities]. *International Journal on Working Conditions, 7*, 68-83.

Silva, I. S., & Prata, J. (2015). Work schedules and human resource management: The case of shift work. In C. Machado & J. P. Davim (Eds.), *Human resource management challenges and changes* (pp. 67-93). New York: Nova Publishers.

Silva, H., & Silva, I. S. (2015). Gestão e adaptação aos horários de trabalho: Um estudo de caso no setor hoteleiro [Management and adaptation to work schedule: A case study in the hospitality sector]. *International Journal on Working Conditions, 9*, 99-116.

Šimunić, A., & Gregov, L. (2012). Conflict between work and family roles and satisfaction among nurses in different shift systems in Croatia: A questionnaire survey. *Arhiv Za Higijenu Rada i Toksikologiju, 63*(2), 189-197.

Smith, C. S., Folkard, S., & Fuller, J. A. (2003). Shiftwork and working hours. In J. C. Quick & L. E. Tetrick (Eds.), *Handbook of occupational health psychology* (pp. 163-183) (2nd ed.). Washington, DC: American Psychological Association.

Smith, L., Macdonald, I., Folkard, S., & Tucker, P. (1998). Industrial shift systems. *Applied Ergonomics, 29*(4), 273-280.

Smith-Coggins, R., Rosekind, M. R., Buccino, K. R., Dinges, D. F., & Moser, R. P. (1997). Rotating shiftwork schedules: Can we enhance physician adaptation to night shifts? *Academic Emergency Medicine, 4*(10), 951-961.

Stimpfel, A. W., Brewer, C. S., Kovner, C. T. (2015). Scheduling and shift work characteristics associated with risk for occupational injury in newly licensed registered nurses: An observational study. *International Journal of Nursing Studies, 52*(11), 1686-93.

Tepas, D. (1993). Educational programmes for shiftworkers, their families, and prospective shiftworkers. *Ergonomics, 36*(1-3), 199-209.

Thierry, H., & Jansen, B. (1998). Work time and behaviour at work. In P. J. D. Drenth, H. Thierry & C. J. de Wolff (Eds.), *Handbook of work and organizational psychology* (Vol. 2: Work Psychology) (2nd ed., pp. 89-119). East Sussex: Psychology Press.

Tucker, P., Smith, L., Macdonald, I., & Folkard, S. (2000). Effects of direction of rotation in continuous and discontinuous 8 hour shift systems. *Occupational and Environmental Medicine, 57*, 678-684.

Tuttle, R., & Garr, M. (2012). Shift work and work to family fit: Does schedule control matter? *Journal of Family Economic Issues, 33*, 261-271.

Wedderburn, A. (1991) (Ed.). *Conseils pour les travailleurs postés. Bulletin européen sur le travail posté.* Dublin: Fondation Européenne pour L'amélioration des Conditions de Vie et de Travail.

Wedderburn, A. (1993). Teaching grandmothers how to suck eggs: Do shiftworkers need rules or guidelines? *Ergonomics, 36*(1-3), 239-246.

Wedderburn, A., & Scholarios, D. (1993). Guidelines for shiftworkers: Trials and errors? *Ergonomics, 36*(1-3), 211-217.

BIBLIOGRAPHY

20 questions & answers about shift work disorder
LCCN	2011282041
Type of material	Book
Personal name	Chokroverty, Sudhansu.
Main title	20 questions & answers about shift work disorder/Sudhansu Chokroverty.
Published/Created	Sudbury, MA: Jones & Bartlett Learning, c2012.
Description	iv, 41 p.; 23 cm.
ISBN	1449621007
	9781449621001
LC classification	RC963.5.S54 C56 2012
Variant title	20 questions and answers about shift work disorder
	Twenty questions & answers about shift work disorder
Subjects	Shift systems--Health aspects--Popular works.
	Work Schedule Tolerance.
	Occupational Diseases.

At the heart of work and family: engaging the ideas of Arlie Hochschild
LCCN	2010021012
Type of material	Book
Main title	At the heart of work and family: engaging the ideas of Arlie Hochschild/edited by Anita Ilta Garey, Karen V. Hansen; foreword by Barbara Ehrenreich.
Published/Created	New Brunswick, N.J.: Rutgers University Press, c2011.

Description	xix, 278 p.; 23 cm.
ISBN	9780813549552
LC classification	HD4904.25 .A8 2011
Related names	Garey, Anita Ilta, 1947-
	Hansen, Karen V.
Contents	Inside the clockwork of male careers/Arlie Russell Hochschild -- Shift work in multiple time zones: some implications of contingent and nonstandard employment for family life/Vicki Smith -- Where families and children's activities meet: gender, meshing work, and family myths/Patricia Berhau, Annette Lareau, and Julie E. Press -- Emotional carework, gender, and the division of household labor/Rebecca J. Erickson -- Why can't I have what I want? Timing employment, marriage, and motherhood/Rosanna Hertz -- Framing couple time and togetherness among American and Norwegian professional couples/Jeremy Schulz -- Love and gratitude: single mothers talk about men's contributions to the second shift/Margaret K. Nelson -- The asking rules of reciprocity/Karen V. Hansen -- Wives who play by the rules: working on emotions in the sport marriage/Steven M. Ortiz -- Emotion work in the age of insecurity/Marianne Cooper -- The crisis of care/Barrie Thorne -- The family work of parenting in public/Marjorie L. DeVault -- Maternally yours: the emotion work of maternal visibility/Anita Ilta Garey -- Invisible care and the illusion of independence/Lynn May Rivas -- Remaking family through subcontracting care: elder care in Taiwanese and Hong Kong immigrant families/Pei-Chia Lan -- The Viacom generation: the consumer child and the corporate parent/Juliet B. Schor -- Consumption as care and belonging: economies of dignity in children's daily lives/Allison J. Pugh -- Interracial intimacy on the commodity frontier/Kimberly McClain DaCosta -- The globalization-family nexus: families as mediating structures of globalization/Nazli Kibria -- Homeland visits:

	transnational magnified moments among low-wage immigrant men/Hung Cam Thai -- Childbirth at the global crossroads/Arlie Russell Hochschild.
Subjects	Hochschild, Arlie Russell, 1940---Criticism and interpretation.
	Work and family.
Notes	Includes bibliographical references.
Series	Families in focus series

Breast cancer epidemiology

LCCN	2009930938
Type of material	Book
Main title	Breast cancer epidemiology/Christopher I. Li, editor; foreword by Janet R. Daling.
Published/Created	New York: Springer, c2010.
Description	xiii, 417 p.: ill. (some col.); 24 cm.
Links	Table of contents only http://www.loc.gov/catdir/toc/fy11pdf04/2009930938.html
ISBN	9781441906847 (hbk.: alk. paper)
	1441906843 (hbk.: alk. paper)
	9781441906854 (e-ISBN)
	1441906851 (e-ISBN)
LC classification	RC280.B8 B6872 2010
Related names	Li, Christopher I-Fu.
Contents	Global burden of breast cancer/Jacques Ferlay ... [et al.] -- Breast cancer biology and clinical characteristics/Amanda I. Phipps and Christopher I. Li -- In situ breast cancer/Brian L. Sprague and Amy Trentham-Dietz -- Endogenous hormones/Amanda I. Phipps and Christopher I. Li -- Exogenous hormones/Christopher I. Li and Elisabeth F. Beaber -- Reproductive factors/Mats Lambe -- Physical activity and anthropometric factors/Katherine D. Henderson, Jennifer Prescott, and Leslie Bernstein -- Diet and nutrition/Martin Lajous and Shumin M. Zhang -- Environmental and occupational exposures/Amanda I. Phipps ... [et al.] -- Shift work and circadian disruption/Scott Davis and Dana K. Mirick -- Non-hormonal medications and chronic diseases/Patricia

	F. Coogan -- Male breast cancer/Ian S. Fentiman -- Inherited predisposition: familial aggregation and high risk genes/Kathleen E. Malone and Kerryn W. Reding -- Common genetic susceptibility loci/Mikkel Z. Oestergaard and Paul Pharoah -- Mammographic density as a potential surrogate marker for breast cancer/Norman F. Boyd, Lisa J. Martin, and Salomon Minkin -- Breast cancer screening/Karla Kerlikowske -- Principles of breast cancer therapy/Allison W. Kurian and Robert W. Carlson -- Breast cancer outcomes/Graham A. Colditz and Courtney Beers.
Subjects	Breast--Cancer--Epidemiology.
	Breast Neoplasms--epidemiology.
	Hormones--adverse effects.
Notes	Includes bibliographical references and index.

Circadian medicine

LCCN	2015004403
Type of material	Book
Main title	Circadian medicine/edited by Christopher S. Colwell, Laboratory of Circadian and sleep medicine, Department of Psychiatry and Biobehavioral Sciences, University of California Los Angeles, Los Angeles, CA, USA.
Published/Produced	Hoboken, New Jersey: John Wiley & Sons Inc., [2015]
Description	xviii, 353 pages: color illustrations; 25 cm
ISBN	9781118467787 (paper)
LC classification	QP84.6 .C555 2015
Related names	Colwell, Christopher S., editor.
Summary	"Circadian rhythms, the biological oscillations based around our 24-hour clock, have a profound effect on human physiology and healthy cellular function. Circadian Rhythms: Health and Disease is a wide-ranging foundational text that provides students and researchers with valuable information on the molecular and genetic underpinnings of circadian rhythms and looks at the impacts of disruption in our biological clocks in health and disease.Circadian

Rhythms opens with chapters that lay the fundamental groundwork on circadian rhythm biology. Section II looks at the impact of circadian rhythms on major organ systems. Section III then turns its focus to the central nervous system. The book then closes with a look at the role of biological rhythms in aging and neurodegeneration. Written in an accessible and informative style, Circadian Rhythms: Health and Disease,will be an invaluable resource and entry point into this fascinating interdisciplinary field that brings together aspects of neuroscience, cell and molecular biology, and physiology"--Provided by publisher.

Contents Machine generated contents note: Part I: Fundamental Concepts Introduction: Colwell 1. Molecular clockwork and the determinants of human circadian clock Steve Brown, University of Zurich, 2. SCN Circuitry with a focus on outputs including ANS, body temperature Rae Silver, Columbia University, Ruud Buijs, Universidad Nacional Autonoma de Mexico 3. Sleep and circadian rhythms: partners in the regulation of behavior. Mistlberger RE, Simon Fraser University, Burnaby, BC, Canada OR T. Deboer, Leiden University, NL 4. Circadian Sleep disorders Phyllis C. Zee, Sleep Disorders Center, Northwestern University OR Derk-Jan Dijk, University of Surrey 5. Sleep and circadian rhythms: reciprocal partners in the regulation of behavior. Mistlberger RE, Simon Fraser University, Burnaby, BC, Canada or T. Deboer, Leiden Univeristy, NL 6. Circadian regulation of arousal and role in chronic fatigue/Mary Harrington, Smith College Part II: Circadian regulation of major organ system 7. Physiology of the adrenal and liver circadian clocks/Henrik Oster, Max-Planck Institute Biophysical Chemistry Goettingen Germany 8. Nutrition and diet as potent regulators of the liver clock. Shigenobu Shibata; Waseda University, Tokyo, Japan; 9. Desynchrony of the human circadian system as a cause of pathophysiology in the heart and pancreas.Frank Scheer, Harvard University, 10. Cardiomyocyte circadian clock OR Circadian Clocks in the Vasculature M.E. Young, University of Alabama; Garret A. Fitzgerald, M.D (University of Pennsylvania) 11. Integration of Circadian Mechanisms and Energy Balance Joseph Bass, Northwestern University 12. Disruption of circadian rhythms and development of diabetes Aleksey V. Matveyenko, University of California Los Angeles 13. Respiratory clocks Hitoshi Okamura, Kyoto University, Japan 14. Circadian clock control of the cellular response to DNA damage and cancer. Sancar, A, University of North Carolina School of Medicine, Chapel Hill, NC Part III: clocks in the central nervous system: 15. Sleep and circadian regulation of vigilance and cognitive performance in humans Ken P Wright, Jr. Center for Neuroscience, University of Colorado, Boulder, CO 16. Circadian clock, reward, and addictive behaviors Albrecht U, University of Fribourg, Fribourg, Switzerland: 17. Circadian rhythms and mood disorders McClung, CA; University of Pittsburgh Medical School, 18. Circadian regulation of memory processes Colwell CS Part IV: Aging and neurodegeneration 19. Is circadian dysfunction an integral symptom of Schizophrenia? Foster RG, University of Oxford, Oxford, UK 20. Alzheimer's disease and the mistiming of behavior. Antle M, University of Calgary, Calgary, Canada 21. Circadian dysfunctional in Huntington's disease Morton AJ, University of Cambridge, Cambridge, United Kingdom 22. The Aging clock Block GD, University of California Los Angeles: 23. Social jet lag and the costs of 24/7 society Till Roenneberg, Ludwig-Maximilians-University Munich 24. How shift work and a destabilized circadian system may increase risk for development of cancer and type 2 diabetes. Eva Schemhammer, Harvard University.

Subjects	Circadian Clocks--physiology.
	Circadian Rhythm--physiology.
	Chronobiology Disorders--etiology.
Notes	Includes bibliographical references (pages 346-349) and index.
Additional formats	Online version: Circadian medicine Hoboken, New Jersey: John Wiley & Sons Inc., [2015] 9781118467794 (DLC) 2015005255

Handbook of sleep medicine

LCCN	2011008449
Type of material	Book
Main title	Handbook of sleep medicine/edited by Alon Y. Avidan, Phyllis C. Zee.
Edition	2nd ed.
Published/Created	Philadelphia: Wolters Kluwer Health/Lippincott Williams & Wilkins, c2011.
Description	xxii, 490 p.: ill.; 21 cm.
ISBN	9781609133474 (pbk.)
	1609133471 (pbk.)
LC classification	RC547 .A86 2011
Related names	Avidan, Alon Y.
	Zee, Phyllis C., 1954-
Summary	"The handbook offers practical and easily referenced algorithmic flow diagrams. It provides the flexibility of a quick, easily referenced guideline whereas the chapters provide specific diagnostic tools and detailed reviews of treatments"--Provided by publisher.
Contents	Sleep disturbances and comorbidities/Phyllis C. Zee and Alon Y. Avidan -- Sleep disordered breathing/Barbara A. Phillips -- Insomnia/David N Neubauer -- Hypersomnia and narcolepsy/Timothy F. Hoban and Ronald D. Chervin -- Parasomnias/Alon Y. Avidan -- Restless legs syndrome and related periodic leg movements of sleep: tips and tools for proper screening and diagnosis/Rachel E. Salas, Russell J. Rasquinha, and Charlene E. Gamaldo -- Circadian rhythm sleep disorders/Cathy Goldstein, Brandon S. Lu, and Phyllis C. Zee -- Management of

	sleep-disordered breathing/Puja Kohli, Richard Schwab, and Atul Malhotra -- Insomnia therapy/David N. Neubauer -- Treatment of central nervous system hypersomnias/Jeffrey H. Lin and Clete A. Kushida -- Management of parasomnias/Rochelle S. Zak, Jorge M. Mallea, and R. Nisha Aurora -- Management of restless legs syndrome and periodic leg movement disorder/Maryann C. Deak and John W. Winkelman -- Circadian rhythm sleep disorders management/R. Robert Auger -- Sleep disorders in children/Katherine Finn Davis and Judith A. Owens -- Diagnosis and treatment of sleep disorders in older adults/Alexandrea Harmell and Sonia Ancoli-Israel -- Sleep in medical disorders/John Harrington, Naveen Kanathur, and Teofilo Lee-Chiong -- Sleep in neurological disorders/Raman K. Malhotra and Alon Y. Avidan -- Sleep and psychiatric disorders/Andrew D. Krystal -- Sleep and pregnancy/Christopher Morgan and Hrayr Attarian -- Shift-work sleep disorder: sleep and performance in medical training/Valentina Gumenyuk and Christopher L. Drake -- Jet lag disorder/Kathryn J. Reid -- Sleep, driving, and the law/Brian Boehlecke.
Subjects	Sleep disorders--Handbooks, manuals, etc. Sleep Disorders--diagnosis--Handbooks. Sleep--physiology--Handbooks. Sleep Disorders--therapy--Handbooks.
Notes	Includes bibliographical references and index.

Sleep deprivation, stimulant medications, and cognition

LCCN	2012029778
Type of material	Book
Main title	Sleep deprivation, stimulant medications, and cognition/edited by Nancy Wesensten.
Published/Created	Cambridge: Cambridge University Press, c2012.
Description	xii, 274 p.: ill.; 26 cm.
ISBN	9781107004092 (hardback: alk. paper)
LC classification	RC548 .S537 2012

Related names Wesensten, Nancy Jo.
Summary "Sleep Deprivation: Stimulant Medications and Cognition provides a review, synthesis and analysis of the scientific literature concerning stimulant medications and neurobehavioral performance, with an emphasis on critically evaluating the practical utility of these agents for maintaining cognitive performance and alertness in sleep-deprived (but otherwise healthy) individuals. The book explores the nature of sleep loss-induced cognitive deficits, neurophysiologic basis of these deficits, relative efficacy and limitations of various interventions (including non-pharmacological), and implications for applying these interventions in operational environments (commercial and military). Readers of this volume will gain a working knowledge of: [bullet] Mechanisms contributing to sleep loss-induced cognitive deficits [bullet] Differential effects of stimulant compounds on various aspects of cognition [bullet] Considerations (such as abuse liability) when applying stimulant interventions in operational settings [bullet] Current state and future directions for including stimulants in comprehensive fatigue-management strategies. This text is key reading for researchers and trainees in sleep and psychopharmacology"--Provided by publisher.

Contents Machine generated contents note: Foreword: sustaining cognitive performance: a modern imperative David Dinges; Part I. Basic Mechanisms: Cognitive Performance and Sleep: 1. The true nature of sleep loss-Induced 'neurocognitive performance deficits' - a critical appraisal Thomas J. Balkin; 2. Using fMRI to study cognitive function and its modulation in sleep deprived persons - a selective overview Michael W. L. Chee and Su Mei Lee; 3. The neurochemistry of cognitive impairment following sleep loss Robert E. Strecker and James T. McKenna; 4. The genetic basis of individual vulnerability to sleep loss Phillip J. Quartana and

Tracy L. Rupp; Part II. Stimulant Reversal of Cognitive Deficits: 5. Modafinil reversal of cognitive deficits during sleep loss Nancy J. Wesensten; 6. Utility of caffeine: evidence from the laboratory Michael H. Bonnet and Donna L. Arand; 7. Caffeine: mechanism of action, genetics and behavioural studies conducted in task simulators and the field Christina E. Carvey, Lauren A. Thompson, Caroline R. Mahoney and Harris R. Lieberman; 8. Stimulants in models of shift work and shift work disorder Jonathan R. L. Schwartz and Aaron M. Henley; 9. The potential for abuse of stimulants in chronically sleep-restricted populations Emma Childs and Harriet de Wit; 10. Cognition enhancers versus stimulants Megan St Peters and Martin Sarter; 11. Novel pathways for stimulant development: the histaminergic system John J. Renger; 12. Novel pathways for stimulant development: the hypocretin/orexin system Ravi K. Pasumarthi and Thomas S. Kilduff; Part III. Alternatives for Sustaining Cognitive Performance During Sleep Loss: 13. Light exposure for improving cognition during sleep loss and circadian misalignment Kenneth P. Wright, Jr, Tina M. Burke and Mark R. Smith; 14. Nutritional countermeasures for cognitive performance decrements following sleep deprivation Caroline R. Mahoney and Harris R. Lieberman; 15. The role of alertness monitoring in sustaining cognition during sleep loss Melissa M. Mallis and Francine O. James; 16. Sustaining neurobehavioral performance on less sleep: is SWS enhancement the key? Janine M. Hall-Porter and James K. Walsh; Part IV. Summary and Conclusions: 17. Use of stimulants in operational settings: issues and considerations Nicholas Davenport, Cheryl Lowry and Brian Pinkston; 18. Fatigue management: the art of the state Tracy L. Rupp, Nancy J. Wesensten and Thomas J. Balkin.

Subjects   Sleep Deprivation.

	Central Nervous System Stimulants--adverse effects.
	Cognition--drug effects.
	Neurobehavioral Manifestations.
Notes	Includes bibliographical references and index.

Sleep, health, and society: from aetiology to public health

LCCN	2010021229
Type of material	Book
Main title	Sleep, health, and society: from aetiology to public health/edited by Francesco P. Cappuccio, Michelle A. Miller, Steven W. Lockley.
Published/Created	Oxford; New York: Oxford University Press, 2010.
Description	xix, 471 p.: ill.; 26 cm.
ISBN	9780199566594 (alk. paper)
	0199566593 (alk. paper)
LC classification	RA786 .S637 2010
Related names	Cappuccio, Francesco.
	Miller, Michelle A., Dr.
	Lockley, Steven W.
Summary	"Sleep disturbances and sleep deprivation are common in modern society. Increasingly populations have been subjected to a steady constant decline in the number of hours devoted to sleep, due to changes in a variety of environmental and social conditions. Through the application of epidemiological methods of investigation sleep deprivation has been shown to be associated with a variety of chronic conditions and health outcomes, detectable across the entire lifespan, from childhood to adulthood to older age. Sleep medicine is rapidly being recognised as a growing area of clinical medicine, affecting wide-ranging specialists including respiratory physicians, neurologists, cardiologists and psychiatrists. However, it also has huge implications in the fields of epidemiology, public health, and preventive medicine. This book summarises for the first time the epidemiological evidence linking sleep deprivation and disruption to several chronic conditions, and explores the public health implications with the view

to developing preventive strategies. It will appeal to both preventive medicine specialists, sleep researchers, and clinicians involved in the various specialities that impact upon this growing field. *About the series*: By looking at public health issues from a unique condition-based approach, the innovative From Aetiology to Public Health series examines top public health issues from aetiology through to public health and prevention. *Future titles in the series*: *Chronic Pain Epidemiology*, edited by P Croft, F Blyth, and D van der Windt *Obesity Epidemiology* edited by D Crawford, R Jeffrey, K Ball, and J Brug *Respiratory Epidemiology*, edited by J Jaakkola, M Jaakkola, G Viegi, and M Eisner"--Provided by publisher.

Contents Machine generated contents note: -- 1. Sleep, health and society: the contribution of epidemiology, *F. P. Cappuccio, M. A. Miller, S. W. Lockley* 2. Principles of sleep physiology, *S. W. Lockley* 3. Sleep deprivation and sleep disruption: risk factors and risk markers, *N. S. Marshall, S. Stranges* 4. Sleep and mortality, *J. E. Ferrie, M. Kivimaki, M. Shipley* 5. The epidemiology of sleep and cardiovascular risk and disease, *F. P. Cappuccio, M. A. Miller* 6. Sleep and metabolic risk and disease, *J. Broussard, K. L. Knutson* 7. Sleep and respiratory disease, *A. Xie, R. Kakkar, M. C. Teodorescu, L. Herpel, V. Krishnan, M. Teodorescu* 8. The epidemiology of sleep and depression, *S. Weich* 9. Sleep and neurological disorders, *D. A. Cohen, A. Roy* 10. Sleep in children, *D. Gozal, K. Spruyt* 11. Sleep, inflammation and disease, *M. A. Miller, F. P. Cappuccio* 12. The genetics of sleep, *M. A. Miller* 13. The sociology of sleep, *S. Williams, R. Meadows, S. Arber* 14. Psychosocial and medical consequences of misinterpreting sleep disturbance, *G. Stores* 15. *Sleep and shift work, J. Axelsson* 16. Sleepiness, alertness and performance, *T. Akerstedt* 17. Effect of lack of sleep on medical errors, *C. P. Landrigan* 18.

	European working time directive and medical errors, F. P. Cappuccio, M. A. Miller 19. A commentary on sleep education, E. Peile 20. Sleep, law and policy, C. B. Jones, C. J. Lee, S. Rajaratnam 21. Ethical considerations for the scheduling of work in continuous operations: physicians in training as a case study, C. Czeisler.
Subjects	Sleep--Health aspects.
	Sleep deprivation.
	Sleep Initiation and Maintenance Disorders--epidemiology.
	Fatigue--complications.
	Sleep Deprivation--complications.
	Sleep Initiation and Maintenance Disorders--prevention & control.
Notes	Includes bibliographical references and index.
Series	From aetiology to public health series
	From aetiology to public health.

Sleep, sleepiness and traffic safety

LCCN	2010027249
Type of material	Book
Main title	Sleep, sleepiness and traffic safety/Joris C. Verster and Charles F.P. George, editors.
Published/Created	New York: Nova Science Publishers, c2011.
Description	xi, 251 p.: ill.; 27 cm.
ISBN	9781617289439 (hardcover)
	1617289434 (hardcover)
LC classification	HE5613.5 .S54 2011
Related names	Verster, Joris C. (Joris Cornelis), 1970-
	George, Charles F. P.
Contents	Sleep, sleepiness, and traffic accidents: an introduction/Shery Goril, Colin M. Shapiro -- Transport, sleepiness and sleep restriction: a major public health issue/P. Philip, P. Sagaspe, J. Taillard -- The role of driver sleepiness in car crashes: a systematic review of epidemiological studies/Jennie Connor -- Characteristics of sleep-related car incidents/Fridulv Sagberg -- Psychophysiological

	characteristics of driver fatigue/Ashley Craig, Yvonne Tran, Nirupama Wijesuriya -- Brain activity during sleepy driving/Christos Papadelis -- Insomnia and traffic safety/J.C. Verster -- Sleep apnea and traffic safety/Charles F.P. George -- Narcolepsy and traffic safety/Monique A.J. Mets, Claire E.H.M. Donjacour, Joris C. Verster -- Shift work/Monique A.J. Mets, Joris C. Verster -- Long-haul truck driving and traffic safety: studying drowsiness and truck driver safety using a naturalistic driving method/Richard J. Hanowski ... [et al.] -- Sleepiness, alcohol and traffic safety/A. Vakulin ... [et al.] -- Countermeasures to driver sleepiness/Elke De Valck -- Mobile societies, automobility and public policy: emerging issues in driver health and society/Henry J. Moller.
Subjects	Traffic safety. Fatigue. Sleep disorders.
Notes	Includes bibliographical references and index.
Series	Transportation issues, policies and R&D Transportation issues, policies and R&D series.

Social and family issues in shift work and non-standard working hours.

LCCN	2016944168
Type of material	Book
Main title	Social and family issues in shift work and non standard working hours.
Published/Produced	New York, NY: Springer Berlin Heidelberg, 2016.
ISBN	9783319422848

The 17 day diet: a doctor's plan designed for rapid results

LCCN	2011281675
Type of material	Book
Personal name	Moreno, Mike, 1968-
Main title	The 17 day diet: a doctor's plan designed for rapid results/Mike Moreno.
Edition	1st Free Press hardcover ed.

Published/Created	New York: Free Press, 2011, c2010.
Description	ix, 243 p.; 24 cm.
Links	Contributor biographical information http://www.loc.gov/catdir/enhancements/fy1113/2011281675-b.html Publisher description http://www.loc.gov/catdir/enhancements/fy1113/2011281675-d.html Sample text http://www.loc.gov/catdir/enhancements/fy1113/2011281675-s.html
ISBN	9781451648652 1451648650
LC classification	RM222.2 .M5683 2011
Variant title	Seventeen day diet
Summary	Presents a revolutionary program adjusts your body metabolically so that you burn fat day in and day out. The program is structured around four 17 day cycles, one of which helps flush sugar and fat storage from your system. Every phase comes with an extensive list of foods, recipes, and sample meal plans to help make grocery shopping a breeze. -- Source other than Library of Congress.
Contents	The 17 day diet. Just give me 17 days; Burn, baby, burn; Cycle 1: accelerate; Cycle 2: activate; Cycle 3: Achieve; Cycle 4: Arrive -- Special considerations. The 17 day cultural diet; The PMS exception diet -- Make it stick. Dining out on the 17 day diet; Family challenges; Surviving holidays; The 17 day diet on the road; Shift work on the 17 day diet; The 17 day diet recipes; Mister M.D., can you please tell me more?
Subjects	Reducing diets. Weight loss. Diet. Weight loss.
Notes	Some versions come with accompanying DVD. Includes bibliographical references (p. 237-242).

The last shift: poems

LCCN	2016012060
Type of material	Book

Personal name	Levine, Philip, 1928-2015, author.
Uniform title	Poems. Selections
Main title	The last shift: poems/Philip Levine.
Edition	First edition.
Published/Produced	New York: Alfred A. Knopf, 2016.
ISBN	9780451493262 (hardcover)
	9780451493774 (softcover)
LC classification	PS3562.E9 A6 2016
Summary	"The final collection of new poems from one of our finest and most beloved poets. The poems in this wonderful collection touch all of the events and places that meant the most to Philip Levine. There are lyrical poems about his family and childhood, the magic of nighttime and the power of dreaming; tough poems about the heavy shift work at Detroit's auto plants, the Nazis, and bosses of all kinds; telling poems about his heroes--jazz players, artists, and working people of every description, even children. Other poems celebrate places and things he loved: the gifts of winter, dawn, a wall in Naples, an English hilltop, Andalusia. And he makes peace with Detroit: "Slow learner that I am, it took me one night/to discover that rain in New York City/is just like rain in Detroit. It gets you wet." It is a peace that comes to full fruition in a moving goodbye to his home town in the final poem in the collection, "The Last Shift.""--Provided by publisher.
Subjects	Poetry/American/General.
Notes	"This is a Borzoi book."
Additional formats	Online version: Levine, Philip, 1928-2015, author. Last shift First edition. New York: Alfred A. Knopf, 2016 9780451493286 (DLC) 2016018517

The neurobiology of circadian timing

LCCN	2012538909
Type of material	Book
Main title	The neurobiology of circadian timing/edited by Andries Kalsbeek ... [et al.].

Edition	1st ed.
Published/Created	Amsterdam; Boston: Elsevier, 2012.
Description	xv, 496 p.: ill., map; 24 cm.
ISBN	9780444594273 (hbk.)
	0444594272 (hbk.)
LC classification	QP355.2 .N4834 2012
Related names	Kalsbeek, A. (Andries)
Contents	How rod, cone, and melanopsin photoreceptors come together to enlighten the mammalian circadian clock -- Melanopsin phototransduction: Slowly emerging from the dark -- Circadian clocks: Lessons from fish -- Two clocks in the brain: An update of the morning and evening oscillator model in Drosophila -- Circadian system from conception till adulthood -- When does it start ticking? Ontogenetic development of the mammalian circadian system -- The circadian output signals from the suprachiasmatic nuclei -- Suprachiasmatic nucleus: Cellular clocks and networks -- Dynamic neuronal network organization of the circadian clock and possible deterioration in disease -- Interaction of central and peripheral clocks in physiological regulation -- Circadian rhythms in white adipose tissue -- Circadian modulation of sleep in rodents -- Local aspects of sleep: Observations from intracerebral recordings in humans -- The circadian clock component PERIOD 2: From molecular to cerebral functions -- Generation of mouse mutants as tools in dissecting the molecular clock -- In search of a temporal niche: Social interactions -- In search of a temporal niche: Environmental factors -- Feedback actions of locomotor activity to the circadian clock -- The impact of the circadian timing system on cardiovascular and metabolic function -- Nutrition and the circadian timing system -- Managing neurobehavioral capability when social expediency trumps biological imperatives -- Noisy and individual, but doable: Shift-work research in humans -- The evolutionary physiology of photoperiodism in

	vertebrates -- A kiss for daily and seasonal reproduction -- Circannual rhythm in the varied carpet beetle, Anthrenus verbasci -- Avian migration: Temporal multitasking and a case study of melatonin cycles in waders.
Subjects	Neurobiology.
	Circadian Rhythm.
	Neurobiologie.
	Rythmes circadiens.
Notes	Includes bibliographical references and index.
Series	Progress in brain research, 0079-6123; v. 199
	Progress in brain research; v. 199. 0079-6123

The siesta and the midnight sun: how our bodies experience time

LCCN	2011508299
Type of material	Book
Personal name	Gamble, Jessa.
Main title	The siesta and the midnight sun: how our bodies experience time/Jessa Gamble.
Published/Created	Toronto, Ont.: Viking Canada, c2011.
Description	vii, 230 p.; 24 cm.
Links	Publisher description http://www.loc.gov/catdir/ enhancements/fy1506/2011508299-d.html Contributor biographical information http://www.loc. gov/catdir/enhancements/fy1506/2011508299-b.html
ISBN	9780670065110
	0670065110
LC classification	QH527 .G34 2011
Summary	In The Siesta and the Midnight Sun, award-winning science writer Jessa Gamble explores the continuing significance of the biological clocks that governed our lives before modern technology annihilated the night. She describes experiments that show both rats and people adhere to a 24-hour schedule even when deprived of daylight. When our days are disrupted by shift work, jet lag or space travel, things go wrong. The disastrous chemical leak at Bhopal, India and the calamitous launch of the Space Shuttle Challenger both were caused partly by sleepless workers.

Subjects	Insomnia is rampant in the Western world. Biological rhythms. Time--Social aspects. Experience.
Notes	Includes index.

The veterans and active duty military psychotherapy progress notes planner

LCCN	2009031714
Type of material	Book
Personal name	Berghuis, David J.
Main title	The veterans and active duty military psychotherapy progress notes planner/by David J. Berghuis, Arthur E. Jongsma, Jr.
Published/Created	Hoboken, N.J.: John Wiley, c2010.
Description	xiv, 394 p.; 28 cm.
ISBN	9780470440971 (pbk.)
LC classification	UH629.3 .B47 2010
Related names	Jongsma, Arthur E., Jr., 1943-
Contents	Adjustment to killing -- Adjustment to the military culture -- Amputation, loss of mobility, disfigurement -- Anger management and domestic violence -- Antisocial behavior in the military -- Anxiety -- Attention and concentration deficits -- Bereavement due to the loss of a comrade -- Borderline personality -- Brief reactive psychotic episode -- Chronic pain after injury -- Combat and operational stress reaction -- Conflict with comrades -- Depression -- Diversity acceptance -- Financial difficulties -- Homesickness/loneliness -- Insomnia -- Traumatic brain injury -- Nightmares -- Opioid dependence -- Panic/agoraphobia -- Parenting problems related to deployment -- Performance-enhancing supplement use -- Phobia -- Physiological stress response -- Post-deployment reintegration problems -- Posttraumatic stress disorder (PTSD) -- Pre-deployment stress -- Separation and divorce -- Sexual assault by another service member -- Shift work sleep disorder -- Social discomfort -- Spiritual and religious issues --

	Substance abuse/dependence -- Suicidal ideation -- Survivor's guilt -- Tobacco use.
Subjects	Veterans--Mental health--United States--Handbooks, manuals, etc.
	Soldiers--Mental health--United States--Handbooks, manuals, etc.
	Psychotherapy--Planning--Handbooks, manuals, etc.
	Psychology, Military--Handbooks, manuals, etc.
Notes	Includes bibliographical references.
Series	PracticePlanners series

Women, work and clothes in the eighteenth-century novel

LCCN	2013004680
Type of material	Book
Personal name	Smith, Chloe Wigston.
Main title	Women, work and clothes in the eighteenth-century novel/Chloe Wigston Smith, University of Georgia.
Published/Produced	Cambridge: Cambridge University Press, 2013.
Description	x, 260 pages: illustrations; 26 cm
ISBN	9781107035003 (hardback: alk. paper)
LC classification	PR858.W6 S75 2013
Contents	Introduction -- The rhetoric and materials of clothes. The ornaments of prose -- Paper clothes -- The practical habits of fiction. Shift work -- Domestic work -- Public work -- Afterword.
Subjects	English fiction--18th century--History and criticism.
	Women in literature.
	Clothing and dress in literature.
	Work in literature.
	Working class in literature.
Notes	Includes bibliographical references (pages 233-254) and index.

RELATED NOVA PUBLICATIONS

CREATIVITY IN WORK PROJECTS AS A FUNCTION OF AFFECTIVE SHIFTS: A PILOT STUDY[*]

Florence Mackay and Giovanni B. Moneta[†]
London Metropolitan University, London, UK

Grounded in personality systems interaction (PSI; Kuhl, 2000) theory, the phoenix model of creativity (Bledow, Rosing, & Frese, 2013) posits that an "affective shift", represented by a decrease in negative affect and an increase in positive affect, will result in more creativity. Bledow and co-workers (2013) found supporting evidence for this model on a general sample of workday self-reported experiences. The present study examined the effects of an affective shift throughout an entire work project, with participants from the same industry, in order to paint a more specific picture of how the hypothesized dynamic process leads to creativity in the workplace. The phoenix model was decomposed in three hypotheses: (H1) increase in positive affect will predict more creativity, (H2) decrease in negative affect will predict more creativity, and (H3) increase in positive affect and decrease of negative affect will

---

[*] The full version of this chapter can be found in *Psychology of Creativity: Cognitive, Emotional, and Social Processes*, edited by Giovanni B. Moneta and Jekaterina Rogaten, published by Nova Science Publishers, Inc, New York, 2016.
[†] Corresponding author: London Metropolitan University, School of Psychology, Room T6-20, Tower Building, 166-220 Holloway Road, London N7 8DB, United Kingdom. Email: g.moneta@londonmet.ac.uk.

interact synergistically in predicting more creativity. The hypotheses were tested controlling for adaptive metacognitive traits, which were found to support the self-regulation of emotions in challenging endeavors (Beer, 2013).

A longitudinal study was undertaken with nine members from the creative staff of a broadcasting organization, with data collected on 18 creative projects lasting from 2 to 12 days. Participants completed online surveys on a twice-daily basis for the duration of the project. The survey comprised the Creative Contribution to the Project (CCP) (Moneta, Amabile, Schatzel, & Kramer, 2010), the I-PANAS-SF (Thompson, 2007), and the Positive Metacognitions and Meta-Emotions Questionnaire (PMCEQ) (Beer & Moneta, 2010). Moreover, end-of-project creativity ratings were collected from participants and their project managers.

The workday survey data were aggregated into mean scores for the first half (time 1) and second half (time 2) of a project. Regression analyses showed that end-of-project manager ratings of output creativity were unrelated to affective shifts, which is inconsistent with all three hypotheses. Moreover, end-of-project participant ratings of creative contribution to the project were unrelated to changes in positive and negative affect, which is inconsistent with H1 and H2, respectively, and the two affective shifts interacted but not in a synergistic way, providing mixed support to H3. ANCOVA modeling of repeated participants' ratings of creative contribution to the project revealed that an increase in positive affect resulted in an increase in creativity, lending support to H1; a decrease in negative affect did not influence creativity ratings, not lending support to H2; the two affective shifts interacted but not in a synergistic way, providing mixed support to H3.

The findings from this pilot study suggest that the phoenix model needs to be expanded to account for the different measures of creativity that one adopts and the dynamic complexity of repeated self-assessments. The implications of these findings and directions for future research are outlined.

Circadian Disruption and Vascular Variability Disorders (VVD): Mechanisms Linking Aging, Disease State and Arctic Shift-Work: Applications for Chronotherapy[*]

D. G. Gubin,[†,1] *G. Cornelissen*[2], *D. Weinert*[3],
A. S. Vetoshkin[4], *L. I. Gapon*[5],
N. P. Shurkevich[5], *F. A. Poshinov*[5],
N. V. Belozerova[5] *and L. A. Danilova*[1]

[1]Department of Biology, Medical Academy, Tyumen, Russia
[2]Halberg Chronobiology Center, University of Minnesota,
Minneapolis, MN, USA
[3]Institute of Zoology, Martin-Luther-University, Halle, Germany
[4]Medical Unit, "Gazprom Dobycha Yamburg"
LLC, Yamburg, Russia
[5]Tyumen Cardiology Center – Branch of Research Institute of Cardiology,
Siberian Branch of the Russian Academy of Medical Sciences,
Tyumen, Russia

In memory of Franz Halberg, the father of chronobiology:
1919-2013

A fast growing body of evidence indicates that the circadian system is important for health. In turn, desynchrony has been associated with the development of numerous age-related diseases and the aging process. Alterations of the circadian variation occurring within the physiological range provide warning signs that, if acted upon, lead to truly primary prevention not across the board but targeted to the individual person. This is the case for instance for Vascular Variability Disorders. Particular attention is given to

---

[*] The full version of this chapter can be found in *Circadian Cardiology with Focus on Both Prevention and Intervention*, edited by Krasimira Hristova, Abdulla Shehab, Germaine Cornelissen and RB Singh, published by Nova Science Publishers, Inc, New York, 2015.

[†] Address for Correspondence: D. Gubin. Tyumen Medical Academy. Odesskaya, 52. 625023 Tyumen. dgubin@mail.ru.

blood pressure and heart rate recorded in the elderly, in shift-workers in the Arctic, and to a personalized chronotherapeutic approach.

WORKING SCHEDULES AND HUMAN RESOURCE MANAGEMENT: THE CASE OF SHIFT WORK[*]

Isabel S. Silva[†] and Joana Prata
School of Psychology, University of Minho, Portugal

This chapter begins by focusing on the structuring role of working time in other spheres of individuals' lives as well as the growing diversity of working time arrangements adopted by organizations. Starting from the literature review about the effects associated with a particular schedule arrangement—shift work—and an empirical study conducted among five Portuguese textile organizations that use this hourly modality, the role that human resource management can assume in this field is discussed. Globally, the ten qualitative interviews conducted in the presented study point to a consensus with the literature regarding the perception of the problems often associated with this organization mode of working time, especially in connection with the night shift. On the other hand, and from the viewpoint of how the management of issues related to shift work is done, the data suggest the existence of variability within the organizations that have adopted these practices. The chapter ends by reflecting on the contribution of flexible practices and worker participation in the management of working time in general and of shift work in particular.

---

[*] The full version of this chapter can be found in *Human Resource Management Challenges and Changes*, edited by Carolina Machado and Professor J. Paulo Davim, published by Nova Science Publishers, Inc, New York, 2014.
[†] Corresponding author: isilva@psi.uminho.pt.

CIRCADIAN DISRUPTION OF SLEEP AND NIGHT SHIFT WORK WITH RISK OF CARDIOVASCULAR DISEASE AND DIABETES[*]

R. B. Singh[†,1], B. Anjum[2], Rajiv Garg[1], Narsingh Verma[3], Ranjana Singh[2], A. A. Mahdi[2], R. K. Singh[4], Fabien De Meester[5], Agnieszka Wilkzynska[5], Suniti Dharwadkar[6], Toru Takahashi[7], Sarrafi Zadeh S[8], Shabnam Omidvor[8] and Douglas W. Wilson[9]

[1]Halberg Hospital and Research Institute, Moradabad, India
[2]Department of Biochemistry, C S M Medical University, India
[3]Department of Physiology, C S M Medical University, India
[4]Department of Biochemistry, SGRRIM &HS, Dehradun India
[5]The Tsim Tsoum Institute, Krakow, Poland
[6]S. B. College of Science, Aurangabad, India
[7] Graduate School of Human Environment Science, Fukuoka Women's University, Japan
[8]Faculty member of Nursing and Midwifery, Department of Babol Medical Sciences University, Iran
[9] School of Medicine and Health, Durham, UK

Background. Epidemiologic evidence indicates that sleep loss may be a novel risk factor for cardiovascular diseases (CVDs); hypertension, coronary artery disease (CAD) and stroke. The increased risk of CVDs is possibly linked to the effect of sleep loss on hormones that play a major role in the central control of blood pressure and heart rate variability, also on angiotensin, cytokines, appetite and energy expenditure as well as sympathetic and vagal activity, melatonin and serotonin.

---

[*] The full version of this chapter can be found in *New Research in Cardiovascular Health*, edited by Ram B. Singh, published by Nova Science Publishers, Inc, New York, 2014.
[†] Address for Correspondence: Prof R B Singh, Halberg Hospital and Research Institute, Civil Lines, Moradabad (UP), India , Email: rbs@tsimtsoum.net

Methods. Internet search and expert opinion from colleagues.

Results. Exposure to light at night disturbs the circadian system with alterations of the sleep/activity patterns and suppression of melatonin and leptin production. Light is the most powerful synchronizer but, when exposure occurs at a time when the body would normally not be exposed to light, (that is, at night), then it disrupts the circadian rhythms. In developed countries, approximately, one fifth of the workers may have disruption of sleep due to night shift and may be unable to tolerate exposure to light during this time. Daily physiological variations include normal circadian rhythms which are interactive and require a high degree of phase positioning to produce subjective feelings of well-being. Disturbances in these activities, may predispose circadian desynchronization, (whether from passage over time zones or from shift rotation), resulting in disturbance of the quantity and quality of sleep leading to hormonal and cardiovascular dysfunction. Shift work can increase the risk of CVD by several interrelated psychosocial, behavioral, and physiological mechanisms. Biological mechanisms are related to the activation of the autonomic nervous system, inflammation, dyslipidemia and glucose intolerance, which may increase the risk for atherosclerosis, metabolic syndrome and insulin resistance resulting in CAD, hypertension and stroke. It is important to promote greater changes in behavioural factors like physical activity, Mediterranean-style diet and meditation apart from providing rotation in shift to cover the loss of sleep.

Conclusions. Disruption of sleep has become a public health problem due to industrialization and urbanization. Strategies to reduce the potential for circadian disruption, including extending the daily dark period, appreciating nocturnal awakening in the dark, using dim red light for night-time necessities, and avoiding frequently rotating shifts. There is a need to have more intensive guidelines on dietary intakes, physical activity and meditation to prevent CVDs among subjects who have significant sleep disruption.

24-HOUR CHRONOMICS OF AMBULATORY BLOOD PRESSURE MONITORING IN ROTATING NIGHT SHIFT WORKERS AND CONTROLS[*]

Baby Anjum[1], Nar Singh Verma[2,†], Sandeep Tiwari[3], Vinod Jain[3], Ranjana Singh[1], Shipra Bhardwaj[2], Qulsoom Naz[2], Abbas A. Mahdi[1], Ram B. Singh[4] and Raj K. Singh[5]

[1]Department of Biochemistry, C S M Medical University, Lucknow, India
[2]Department of Physiology, C S M Medical University, Lucknow, India
[3]Department of Surgery, C S M Medical University, Lucknow, India
[4]Halberg Hospital and Research Institute, Moradabad, India
[5]Department of Biochemistry, SGRRIM & HS, Dehradun, India

Background: Concerns about the health of night shift workers has long been debated. Shift work is associated with the disruption of circadian rhythms, where a person's internal body clock is in conflict with the rotating night shift schedule which causes internal desynchronization, sleep disturbances resulting in to increased risk of cardiovascular diseases and diabetes and other physiological disorders.

Objectives: We investigated the circadian pattern of blood pressure and heart rate in night shift workers and day shift controls, and whether the changes in circadian pattern produced by rotating night shift are reversible in due course of time.

Method: 14 healthy nursing professionals, aged 20-40 year, performing day and night shifts and 14 subjects as controls, performing day duty were recruited in the study. Circadian patterns of blood pressure and heart rate were evaluated in night shift workers during the work shift (Night & Day shift) and in controls.

---

[*] The full version of this chapter can be found in *Cardiovascular Health and Chronomics*, edited by Ram B. Singh, published by Nova Science Publishers, Inc, New York, 2014.
[†] Address correspondence to: Dr N S Verma, Professor. Department of Physiology, C S M Medical University (Formerly King George's Medical University), Lucknow-226003 (Uttar Pradesh) India. E-mail: drnsvermakgmu@gmail.com; Phone: +91 9839064560 Fax No: 0522-2257539.

Result: Night shift workers showed a very interesting altered circadian pattern of double amplitude when subject went back to the day shift. An extremely significant different pattern of SBP and DBP double amplitude was found between day shift and controls (p<0.01).

Conclusion: Effect of rotating night shift develops later due to rotating shift and desynchronization. Acrophase pattern was clinically significant when studied in individual subjects in different shifts with controls. Alterations in Acrophase were persistent during night as well as day shift due to incomplete recovery and ecphasia was very common among night shift workers.

INDEX

A

arrhythmia, vii, viii, 23, 32, 33, 43
arterial age, 43
arterial stiffness, vii, viii, 23, 31, 34, 41, 43
atherosclerosis, 25, 30, 31, 35, 38, 40, 42, 43, 94

B

behavior of children, 10
behaviors, 10, 17, 18, 37, 40, 74
blood pressure, 27, 31, 32, 35, 36, 43, 92, 93, 95
body mass index (BMI), 11, 19, 27, 29, 30, 33, 37, 38, 39, 42

C

cardiac arrhythmia, vii, viii, 23
cardiovascular diseases, vii, viii, 23, 24, 26, 30, 93, 95
cardiovascular disorders, vii, viii, 23, 26, 28, 30, 31, 35
cardiovascular morbidity, 25, 26
cardiovascular risk, v, viii, 23, 24, 26, 27, 29, 34, 35, 38, 40, 80
childcare, 4, 8, 15
circadian rhythms, viii, 24, 35, 72, 73, 94, 95
coronary heart disease, vii, viii, 23, 30, 33, 37, 38, 39, 42

D

dyslipidemia, viii, 24, 25, 29, 30, 94

E

employees, ix, 6, 7, 16, 24, 26, 31, 32, 33, 45, 47, 49, 50, 51, 54, 55, 56, 59, 64
employers, 50
employment, 16, 19, 24, 26, 27, 70
employment status, 16
endothelial dysfunction, viii, 24, 25, 26, 28, 34, 35
Europe, 16, 24, 26
European Community, 48
European Union, 3, 18, 46, 63
everyday life, 17, 58
exposure, 28, 33, 78, 94

F

families, ix, 4, 6, 10, 11, 18, 45, 55, 66, 70

family conflict, vii, viii, 2, 6, 7, 9, 15, 16, 17, 19, 61, 64
family life, 2, 5, 6, 7, 18, 21, 30, 60, 70
flexibility, 4, 5, 13, 15, 16, 24, 57, 58, 75

H

human resource management, 20, 46, 57, 59, 61, 64, 66, 92
human resources, ix, 15, 45, 47, 56, 57, 58, 59
hypertension, vii, viii, 23, 25, 26, 30, 31, 32, 33, 40, 93, 94

I

individual characteristics, 58, 61
industrialization, 94
industrialized countries, 12
industry, 18, 19, 24, 37, 46, 59, 62, 63, 65, 89
inflammation, viii, 24, 28, 30, 38, 80, 94
inflammatory responses, 36
intervention, viii, ix, 2, 15, 16, 20, 45, 47, 55, 60, 61, 63, 66
intervention strategies, ix, 16, 45, 55

J

job dissatisfaction, 39, 50
job satisfaction, 6, 26, 27, 50
job strain, 25, 34, 36

L

leisure time, 17, 19

M

management, ix, 2, 9, 15, 16, 35, 45, 46, 47, 52, 54, 56, 57, 58, 59, 66, 76, 77, 78, 87, 92

metabolic syndrome, 27, 30, 37, 38, 41, 94
metabolism, 29, 30, 31, 37, 40
mortality, viii, 23, 24, 26, 27, 34, 43, 80
myocardial infarction, 34, 37, 42

N

napping, 32, 46, 52, 53, 54, 55, 63
narcolepsy, 75

O

obesity, 11, 17, 25, 26, 27, 28, 29, 30, 31, 37, 39, 40, 41, 80
occupational health, ix, 15, 18, 21, 45, 62, 66
overweight, 11, 17, 19, 26, 27, 29, 33, 35, 39

P

Pearson correlations, 60
premature ventricular contractions, 32

Q

QT interval, 33, 36, 40, 43

R

risk factors, vii, viii, 23, 25, 26, 29, 30, 34, 35, 38, 39, 80

S

shift systems, ix, 3, 7, 13, 21, 45, 46, 47, 48, 57, 62, 63, 66
shift work, v, vii, viii, ix, 1, 2, 3, 4, 5, 6, 7, 8, 10, 12, 13, 15, 16, 17, 18, 19, 20, 21, 22, 23, 24, 25, 26, 27, 28, 29, 30, 31, 32, 33, 34, 35, 37, 38, 39, 41, 42, 43, 45, 46, 47, 49, 50, 52, 53, 54, 55, 56, 57, 58, 59,

60, 61, 62, 63, 64, 65, 66, 69, 74, 78, 80, 82, 84, 86, 92, 93, 95, 96
sleep duration, 29, 31, 41, 42
smoking, 26, 27, 33, 36, 37, 38, 39, 41
social isolation, 26, 30
social life, v, vii, viii, ix, 1, 2, 6, 12, 18, 19, 21, 45, 52, 62
stroke, vii, viii, 23, 30, 34, 37, 38, 93, 94

T

training, ix, 16, 45, 46, 47, 55, 56, 57, 76, 80
type 2 diabetes mellitus, 28, 29, 43

U

United States (USA), 4, 26, 87

V

very low density lipoprotein, 29

W

well-being, 5, 7, 10, 15, 17, 19, 21, 48, 49, 94
work schedules, viii, 2, 3, 4, 7, 8, 9, 10, 11, 12, 13, 16, 17, 18, 19, 20, 21, 24, 34, 55
workers, vii, viii, ix, 1, 2, 3, 4, 5, 6, 7, 8, 10, 12, 13, 14, 15, 16, 17, 18, 19, 24, 26, 27, 28, 29, 30, 31, 32, 33, 34, 35, 36, 37, 38, 39, 40, 41, 43, 45, 48, 49, 50, 51, 52, 53, 54, 55, 56, 57, 58, 59, 60, 61, 62, 63, 64, 86, 89, 92, 94, 95, 96
work-family conflict, vii, viii, 2, 6, 7, 9, 15, 16, 17, 61
working conditions, 20, 40, 61, 65
working groups, 15
working hours, vii, viii, 1, 2, 3, 6, 7, 8, 9, 10, 11, 16, 21, 33, 41, 46, 57, 61, 66, 82
workload, 50
workplace, 26, 29, 35, 39, 40, 52, 53, 54, 56, 89